CLIMB
ANOTHER
MOUNTAIN

BY
DONNA S. THOMAS

Blessings
Donna Thomas

1/20/08

D1446207

Warner Press

Arthur M. Kelly, Publication Coordinator
Cover and Layout by Curtis Corzine and Virginia L. Wachenschwanz

Charles F. Thomas

DEDICATION

To my teammate and husband, Chuck Thomas, who was always looking for the next mountain and was never afraid to climb it. He gave me the "fire" to complete the work he would have done had he been here in the flesh and that we could have done together.

TABLE OF CONTENTS

ACKNOWLEDGMENTS

I extend my sincere and heartfelt gratitude to all of the individuals who have been part of the experiences described in this book. They continually spurred me on to higher mountains, with the goal of being more productive for the Lord. I thank Holly Miller, creative writing professor at Anderson University, Anderson, Indiana, for her support, guidance, publishing advice, and encouragement. And I especially thank Karen Roberts, my excellent personal editor, who kept me on track. She helped make this book readable, working hard with me on every page.

INTRODUCTION

We were getting acquainted and chatting as we sat there on the flight to Cincinnati. I mentioned that I was writing a book and her response was, "What is your book about?"

Here was my chance to give her a glimpse of what you are about to experience as you read on.

This book is meant to be inspirational, to show you how prospects, challenges, and even problems can give you the opportunity to walk more closely with God and to seek his plan and his miracles in your life as you move on. We all have to make choices—choices to move forward or to give up, to serve or to be served, to seek God's guidance or go our own way, to praise God or to grumble, to climb the mountain set before us or to look for the lower road.

I trust you can see beyond the stories and into your personal opportunities to climb your mountains and to leave a rich legacy behind you in bringing others to the joy of knowing and following Christ.

Donna S. Thomas

FOREWORD

In this book Donna Thomas deals with decades of front-line, risk-taking, swim, or sink, in the trenches, relationship-building missions.

Real missions, biblical missions, early church apostle-type missions have not been an equal member in our churches' family of programs today. Most believers, if asked, would agree that there is a relationship between a gut-level commitment to world missions and the spiritual life of the individual, a congregation, or a denomination. However, the average Christian's commitment to and demand for more and more self-serving church programming continues to choke the life, relevance, creativity, vitality, meaning, and fulfillment that comes from actively pursuing Christ's Great Commission.

This book is not simply a story. It is Chuck and Donna Thomas's life, pilgrimage, heartbeat, and life assignment. It captures the two indisputable prerequisites for meaningful and fulfilling living: vision and passion. Once they were traditional pastors doing ministry as usual. Then God opened their eyes and touched their spirits. From that day on, a different and consuming dimension of Christian service totally redirected their energies. It made the world their parish and pushed them into faith-stretching endeavors of Christian witness, cross bearing, and heroic living.

I have had the privilege of observing firsthand some of their labors in Mexico, Guatemala, Panama, Nicaragua, and many other areas where they have responded to the marching orders of God, his Word, and his Spirit,

This book is readable, informative, and instructive. It moves with feeling and drama. It shares their fears, cares, and tears, and it shows the joy of seeing the sun break through the fog of circumstances and challenges. It proves that every mountain has its miracles and every spiritual assignment has its divine provisions.

Climb Another Mountain helps the whole Church to recapture its assignment. It is good reading for pulpit, classrooms, and small groups. It confirms that we do not test the resources of God until we attempt the impossible. It calls every believer to experience the joy and thrill that come from allowing God to steer his or her life. Song writer Mary Brown affirmed this when she turned her commitment into the following prayer:

> *"I'll go where you want me to go, dear Lord,*
> *O'er mountain or plain or sea:*
> *I'll say what you want me to say, dear Lord,*
> *I'll be what you want me to be."*

C. Milton Grannum EdD, PhD
New Covenant Church of Philadelphia
Philadelphia, PA

CHAPTER 1
CHOICES: CROSSING THE RIO GRANDE

When you invite a guest to dinner you don't expect him to tell you what to do. Yet there we were—my husband Chuck; our three boys, Mark, Paul, and John; and me—with evangelist Larry DeShay, who was with us for a week while he conducted meetings at our church. Larry enlivened our dinners by telling colorful stories about Guatemala and Mexico. He taught the boys to say, "Please pass the *pan* (bread)," or "Pass the *mantequilla* (butter), *por favor* (please)." As a mother, I was thrilled for their language lesson.

One evening he put his hand on my husband's shoulder and said, "Young man, if you ever want to amount to anything for the Lord, you need a heart for missions."

What is he talking about? I thought with a bit of irritation. *We have enough to do!*

In truth, we knew little about missions in 1961, much less had a heart for it. Why should we? Just eight years earlier, we started our church in Wichita, Kansas, shortly after Chuck finished seminary. It took tremendous effort to grow the congregation from the seventeen members who helped us start to the 250 we had by the early '60s. It was all-consuming. Now Larry was confronting us with a *new* dimension of ministry; it seemed excessive.

Christmas was coming and we planned to take a family trip between Christmas and New Year's Day. The evangelist challenged us to go to Mexico and observe some mission work there. Maybe we should. I was always looking for things to do as a family. This appeared to be a great way to combine things:

family fun, missions awareness, and exposing the boys to a foreign country with a different language and all the educational bells and whistles that warmed a mother's heart. Plus, it would cost a lot less than going to Europe, important factor for a family on a pastor's salary.

It was decision time. Do we say yes to trying something new, unknown, and different—or not? We decided to try it.

It's amazing how the Lord shows us what to do, one step at a time. What grand and wonderful plans he has for us, plans we may never experience if we don't have the courage to take that first step.

Our first step was a big one—across a river.

Our First Rio Grande

When the day arrived to go to Mexico, we loaded our blue station wagon to the bursting point and off we went—unaware that we'd never be the same again.

Driving from Wichita through Oklahoma and Texas was no problem. But as we approached the United States border at the Rio Grande, we suddenly realized that we were leaving the security of our own culture and entering a completely new world; it was our first such venture and it was unsettling. Our fears were myriad: *These people don't understand English! Their ways are different; their food is different. We have to obtain a permit just to enter their country. We can't read the road signs.* Going through the large industrial city of Monterrey, Mexico, the surroundings heightened our awareness that we were among people to whom we couldn't relate.

Our destination was a mission in Saltillo operated by our friend Raymond Hastings. We headed west through the mountains, not knowing our car was low on transmission fluid. Halfway up those peaks, it started acting up.

"Donna, there's something wrong." Chuck's words jolted me. "We've got a problem," he continued.

"What do you think it is?" I asked.

"Well, I'm guessing it might be the transmission."

We felt so alone, and at that point in our journey we were actually *afraid* that some Mexican might stop to help us. Talk about culture shock! Fortunately no one came to our aid. Chuck managed to coax our old station wagon along until we arrived at the mission.

At the mission station, *La Buena Tierra* (The Good Land), our friend Raymond took us to an auto repair shop. The "shop" consisted of an adobe wall around a bare lot. Raymond assured us this was the place, so we stood by as he explained our situation to the mechanic and gave him our keys. Later, when we stopped to check on our car, we discovered that the mechanic had all the parts to be repaired laying on different rocks. Neither Chuck nor I was at all sure our little car would ever run again!

A little while later and much to our *gringo* surprise, the mechanic finished—and even loaded our car with *his* family members for a successful test drive.

This incident was the first of many the Lord used to open our eyes to life on the other side of the Rio Grande. Among the villagers in small churches in the *pueblos* of Jamé and Derramadero, we recognized familiar melodies of the hymns they sang even if we didn't understand the words they used. The experience was heartwarming; we could feel the Spirit of the Lord there. It became obvious to us that the Lord was on the south side of the Rio Grande as well as the north. God must be able to understand Spanish! We had a great time discovering cultural differences and similarities, all while building relationships with such wonderful people. We didn't know it then, but we were like Alice in Wonderland after she stepped through the looking-glass. We were heading for even greater adventures and were no more aware of them than Alice was of hers.

Reentry

Returning home from that first trip to Mexico, our excitement mounted about our experiences. We could hardly wait to tell our congregation all that happened. We worshiped in wonderful church services where we didn't understand the language but could feel the presence of the Lord. We met such outstanding Mexican pastors in those remote little villages. When we stopped at the Bible school, we were so amazed at the energetic and ambitious young people studying to better serve the Lord. They were all very committed and thoroughly friendly. Their "poverty" (at least that's how our Yankee eyes saw their living situation) didn't seem to limit their contentedness. They graciously welcomed us—foreigners in their home.

As we drove, we reflected on what we learned. God indeed wanted us to have a heart for missions. We could never forget those wonderful people, even if we couldn't understand their Spanish. Getting our papers out (we presented passports and drivers licenses to prove our American citizenship and right to reenter the country) at the Rio Grande United States Customs Station and crossing back into Texas increased our level of excitement about the new culture we encountered. We sensed a new burden in our hearts for helping Mexicans reach more of their people for Christ. We were changed. We were sure our friends at home would share our enthusiasm.

More unexpected encounters were ahead of us; fortunately, the Lord was helping us in the process. As soon as we got home we started telling others—or rather, *trying* to tell them. But all they seemed to hear was, "Let me tell you about our vacation," and then they hurriedly countered with tales of their own trips to some place or another. It was frustrating; it seemed as if some horrible competition between people to see who had the best vacation! No one appeared to understand that this wasn't just another trip for us; it was not some picture-postcard-come-to-life. This was a new vision, an overwhelming call to service, and a challenge that set our hearts afire. It was God's calling.

Of course the congregation was a captive audience in our services. A few members looked mildly interested in hearing more; however, when Chuck related in detail our experiences and what the Lord put on his heart about the importance of missions, the church board was *not* interested. Let me repeat, not interested.

One of the board members, Icle McTaggart, summed it up: "Missions? Who cares about missions?" At that point Icle was no more aware of the value of missions than Chuck and I were before our trip.

We were puzzled and frustrated. If the Lord opened our eyes and hearts to his mission field, how were we to help our congregation and church board feel and respond in the same way?

Here we faced another choice: Would we accept our congregation and board's apathetic response, or would we find a way to change it? Was this a closed door or an opportunity for another adventure?

Taking the Church Along

Chuck and I decided that our congregation needed to journey to Mexico to see for themselves how special those people really were and to witness, as we had, that the Lord was very present on the south side of the Rio Grande. We suggested that if our members would arrange to take personal vacation time, we could make the trip a more special occasion by traveling together on a bus. But with one thousand miles from Wichita to Monterrey, what kind of bus could we get to travel safely, yet allow a tolerable amount of personal space for such a long journey?

We found a forty-passenger Continental Trailways bus that was just going out of commercial service. We could purchase the bus for $3,500; the only problem was, we didn't have that kind of money. That amount was equivalent to about half of our yearly salary. But with the help of a loan we became proud owners of a bus. One of the men in our congregation was a mechanic with Trailways, and when he volunteered to drive the bus, his offer confirmed our plans. Soon it was in condition to carry all those people in our congregation who were ready for an adventure.

It's one thing to take our family to Mexico; it is quite another to take a *busload* of people. The biggest challenge: We still didn't know Spanish. How could we handle a large group without *someone* knowing how to communicate well? We feared we could really face trouble without some expert help. Searching for options, we called Gulf Coast Bible College in Houston (now known as Mid-America Bible College in Oklahoma) because we heard some Mexican students were enrolled. They put us in contact with a young man from Monterrey named Enrique Cepeda.

Chuck called Enrique and invited him to Wichita so he could meet us; we planned on inviting him to be our interpreter for the trip. Enrique was a delightful young man. He had the entire summer available, so he came up in June and helped us plan the trip and even did some odd jobs for Chuck with the additional time.

During the planning stage, Enrique challenged us: "Why don't you go further than Monterrey and Saltillo? You really ought to see the national capital, Mexico City. I can help you with that, too." (He had an added incentive. His girlfriend, Lydia, was in Mexico City and it offered them an opportunity to see each other.)

At last, on July 5, 1964, a bus full of Kansans looking for a vacation adventure pulled out of the Pawnee Avenue Church parking lot in Wichita heading south on I-35 for Mexico. Chuck and I watched each passenger as we reached Laredo, Texas, and anticipated their first reaction at their crossing of the Rio Grande. This was exciting for us. We wondered what all thirty-eight of them were expecting.

Arriving in Monterrey, Enrique extended his family's hospitality to our group. Most of our people were able to stay on cots in the Cepeda's house—right in the middle of the city which was a wonderful experience. Along with his sisters, Adamina and Olga, and his brothers, Salvador and Eleazar, Enrique acquainted us with the culture, language, and perhaps best of all the food.

To welcome us, Enrique's mother fixed a beautiful and delicious Mexican meal. It was quite elaborate, and all was well received until someone heard that the meat they were eating was goat. Whoa! No one wanted that, and as readily as they started eating, they stopped. Since no one had eaten goat before, that much "culture" so quickly was not comfortable. Nonetheless, Enrique's mother was a resourceful woman and was not about to waste all that good meat; the next day she prepared it differently in another delicious meal. Our group never knew that they ate goat anyway. I'm sure I could see "mom" Cepeda chuckling all during that meal!

Enrique was a wonderful guide and a great teacher of the Spanish language and Mexican culture. He also was God's instrument; God placed a man in our lives who would serve us, and whom we could serve, as we followed the Lord's new direction for us. After that first congregational trip in the summer of 1964, we worked with Enrique many times in several capacities. He completed his degree work at Gulf Coast, earned another bachelor's degree from Warner Pacific College in Portland, Oregon, received his master's degree from Asbury Theological Seminary in Kentucky, and finally gained his doctorate from Fuller Theological Seminary in California. During those years of schooling, he spent many summers at our home helping us and we in turn helped him.

This dynamic young Mexican later became the dean of a seminary in Mexico City. Next he planted a large church, *Dios es Amor* (God is Love), in Mexico City. In 1996 Enrique established an extremely effective ministry known as *Doulos,* which provides training for lay leaders and pastors across Latin America in evangelism and discipleship. Because of that initial church trip and the doors that opened for us to work together again and again, our friendship with Enrique developed into a "family" relationship; I am known as the American grand-mother to his daughters. It's a special gift from God.

That first bus trip spawned another, and soon another. People in our congregation were signing up to be a part of the next group. We even had people come from other states wanting to join us. Each mission experience was a joyful adventure that everyone wanted to share. God used these trips to open the eyes and hearts of our church family to missions, as God had in our immediate family. During the next two years we probably took half of our congregation of then three hundred fifty people to Mexico.

They, too, were coming home changed.

As for the church board member who asked, "Missions? Who cares about missions?"—he eventually came along and the Lord opened his eyes. To this day Icle is a staunch supporter of getting the Word of God to other countries and cultures. His growing concern about what the Lord is doing in Mexico and Latin America is apparent constantly.

I often wonder what would have happened if we declined the challenge to go to Mexico. Or if we hadn't risked buying that bus on a meager salary. It's easy to look back now and laugh and say we did it right, but where would we be if we had not taken those risks?

Expect the Unexpected

Some years later after that first Rio Grande trip, we sent a busload of people into El Salvador. We forgot to tell the group leader to have "a little something" to give to the border patrols along the way. It's standard procedure there, and people use anything of value instead of money, which is in short supply.

In Mexico they call it *la mordida* (the bite, as in dog bite). It can be quite interesting: people "gift" the inspectors with tomatoes, chickens, cigarettes, or whatever they can spare. Had we remembered to brief our team members on this point, it would have prevented them from having to get out every time they hit a checkpoint, unload all their luggage, and even on occasion—when the inspectors were feeling picky—remove all the seats in the bus for a "customs inspection."

Our group began to get bogged down with these unexpected hassles. The only extra things the group carried on board were a bunch of blue plastic bedpans for the clinic in Nicaragua. What could they give? Our ingenious leader had the answer. When the guards asked, "What are those for?" the group leader answered, "They make marvelous hats they keep the sun out of your eyes. Would you like one?" He tried it on the next guard they encountered. It worked! For a short time, border guards all along that route were proudly wearing blue plastic hats, oblivious to the normal use of those bedpans. In a tropical country where the sun beats down mercilessly, it was just what the doctor ordered!

Crossing Your Rio Grande

This process of crossing the Rio Grande is a continual thing. Not just for Chuck and me, or for our church, but for everyone. It is part of the process of life itself; it's choosing to leave your comfort zone and move into the unknown. Our first Rio Grande was the family trip to Mexico. Another's may be something else. It is easily recognized when we become willing to risk following God's leading regardless of where that may be. Where would Joshua have been when the Israelites wanted to go into the Promised Land, if he hadn't risked stepping into the Jordan River? Or, where would David have been if he decided that tending sheep was all he could ever do? David certainly didn't know anything about fighting a giant. A man the size of Goliath was a life-threatening risk for a young boy. Did he second-guess picking up those stones to use in his slingshot? Like Joshua, David had to *choose* to take that risk. We do too.

Opportunities to follow the Lord, or adventures, as I prefer to call them, appear at various points in our lives. Sometimes we don't recognize them as such. We certainly don't know all that lies ahead as we take that first step. This is what makes it so exciting. If we already knew, we might be intimidated or frightened. Inside all of us is that spirit of adventure and longing to do something different ... out of the ordinary ... to make a difference in this world. Like Alice, we want to move from the status quo and step through the looking-glass. Our step to cross the Rio Grande got us started in the right direction and looking at the world with a new perspective.

Chuck and I certainly didn't know it then but the Lord was preparing us for a new path. This was the embryo for a mission ministry that we would later incorporate and call Project Partner.

We were beginning to see the need to involve churches and Christian believers in a hands-on experience of helping nurture Christians to reach out to others in their own country. We saw the need to join our hands and hearts with native leaders, giving them the boost they needed to spread the Gospel.

The Lord has so many adventures ahead if we say yes to opportunities that seem to come from nowhere. I always tell our sons, "If you want an exciting, fulfilling life, just do what the Lord wants you to do; you will be both pleased and surprised. You never know when something extra special is going to pop up. And you never know all the results that it will bring."

CHAPTER 2
FAITH: LOOKING AND LEAPING

L ooking back at the past is so much easier than trying to see into the future. With hindsight, everything that happened before seems so simple and so right you can see the hand of God at work and review your responses, good or bad, with relative objectivity. But when you're in the trenches of the moment, the luxury of clarity and detached analysis just isn't available. Emotions become a major factor, too. Given those realities, I still wonder how we ever summoned enough faith to buy that forty-passenger airplane.

Until 1968, the Trailways bus continued to serve as the main transportation for our mission trips into Mexico. Then the Lord started stretching us again. It began with another challenge from another pastor: our friend insisted we should see beyond Mexico to all of Central and South America and even the Caribbean islands.

Wow, we thought. *What can we do? How can we do that? It would take an airplane, but where will we get the money for something like that? And who will fly it? All the regulations for airplanes will require us to assume the responsibilities of a corporation, because the church won't want that burden. How can we handle all of this?* We didn't know any of the answers then, but we knew it wasn't going to be easy. With three boys and a church that expected our attention, expanding our ministry would surely require a lot more money than what we presently earned. Additionally, not too many Americans journeyed to Central and South America in the '60s, so we expected some major difficulties.

I asked my parents to come to Wichita and stay with the boys for a couple of weeks. Chuck talked to the church board and the members agreed to give us some time off from our pastoral duties to explore our options. We searched for the money for our "exploratory" trip, and the Lord supplied that, too. Right after Easter in 1968 Chuck and I packed our bags and went to see what was happening beyond Mexico. I'll admit I was nervous; this was a big step for someone once afraid to cross the Rio Grande.

Looking at the Mountain

Chuck and I were never typical tourists, but the Lord made this trip much more interesting than any tourist excursion, even if we'd wanted it to be one. Our first stop was Panama. Missionaries Dean and Nina Flora received us warmly and made sure that we experienced enough to gain a sense for the hearts of the people. We enjoyed visiting churches on both sides of the isthmus, from Panama City to Colon. Seeing all the beautiful children, eating the unique, delicious foods, and just learning about this culture was intriguing and important to the development of our new vision.

The Panama Canal was an especially educational stop, as we discovered how vital it is to Panama's economy. As so many monstrous ships decorated with flags from many different countries passed through the locks, we realized the world was much bigger than we knew. Our view of the world was rapidly expanding.

Ever heard of the San Blas Islands? We hadn't either, but we learned they are off the coast of Panama in the Caribbean, home to the Cuna Indians. These three hundred sixty-five islands are bound together by their common Cuna heritage. At the time of our travel few foreigners ever visited these islands and no foreigner was allowed to stay overnight. Dean made arrangements for us to fly over to the island grouping in a small Cessna 180 airplane; he wanted us to see what God was doing among the inhabitants. That half-hour flight gave us a wonderful view of

Panama. Our panoramic view included vast jungles, mountains, and lakes; we could see the Atlantic and Pacific Oceans at the same time.

Our plane landed on a small runway strip on the island of Nalunaga (Red Snapper). There wasn't too much to the island: palm trees, bamboo huts, and a boat dock. Dean took us over to the biggest hut, which was the meeting place for the island chief and his council. They were inside, waiting for us.

When we entered, we were surprised to see the chief and his council waiting for us in typical Cuna style: reclining in their hammocks! Each one had his own special hammock, and we learned all business was conducted while resting in them. There were three empty hammocks waiting for Dean, Chuck, and me. It made an interesting conference center.

The Cunas were not accustomed to having foreign guests and wanted to extend to us a special welcome. The chief asked lots of questions about us, like where we were from, and what we knew about Jesus. They seemed very eager to learn more about the Lord. Their knowledge of the rest of the world was equally limited—if not more so—and this opportunity presented them with a chance to learn.

We were a unique sight to the Cuna. Chuck, more than six feet tall, created a lot of laughter and finger-pointing from the kids as we walked among the huts. But they were unique to us as well. Women, especially, had striking features and clothing. They each wore a nose ring and had a black line painted down the bridge of their noses to make them appear longer, a sign of beauty in their culture (similar to the reason why we use make-up in our culture). Their blouses featured interesting patterns of reverse appliqué depicting important aspects of their culture. Skirts were simply a piece of material tied around their waists, and red shawls covered their heads. The little girls all wore panties, the little boys nothing at all. Their means of sustenance relied on fishing and growing a little corn on the mainland of Panama, crossing the water in their boats to plant and tend to their crops there, since space was so scarce on the islands. Their meals were simple: roasted fish, corn, rice, coffee and bread. Their system of exchange was mostly barter.

Dean took us over to a bamboo hut, as nondescript as the others. Inside we saw a few boards to sit on, and we soon understood that this was their church. The Cuna Indians knew Jesus. As we worshiped with them in their little bamboo church, we saw them as our brothers and sisters in the family of God. They certainly didn't look like our congregation at home but we gained a warm appreciation for their uniqueness. We formed a fond relationship that gave us real joy and a greater understanding of the Kingdom of God.

As we spent time among the people, we learned how the Cunas had met Jesus. The story was as unique as the Cunas themselves, but the Lord is creative, as we quickly discovered. God used a fisherman (sound familiar?) named Jimmy.

At the beginning of World War II, Jimmy was working on a merchant ship in a New York harbor. A shipmate for several years, he had the opportunity to learn English before he returned home to Nalunaga. Then in 1959 a new missionary came to Panama: Dean Flora. Dean heard about the San Blas islands from a seat companion on the PanAm plane that brought them to Panama. Within four months Dean met Jimmy. Actually, Jimmy Harris was a borrowed name from a friend back on that merchant ship; we never knew his Indian name.

Jimmy's little boy, Freddy, became very ill and Jimmy asked Dean to bring a doctor to Nalunaga to examine his son. The next day, a Christian doctor visited the island to see the boy and leave him some medicine. Freddy was seriously ill, but after Dean and the doctor left, the local Medicine Man told Jimmy to throw the medicine away. The Medicine Man had *better* potions for him. In three days Freddy was dead. Jimmy went to Dean and said, "I loved little Freddy but God knows all this. Let's pray about it," and Jimmy prayed to God. Jimmy realized that the Medicine Man's decision had killed his little boy. The Cunas wouldn't let the Medicine Man back on the island, they were ready to find Christ, the true Healer. Jimmy was the first one who chose to become a Christian.

Jimmy was well-liked and greatly respected among all the Cuna Indians, not just by those on his island. So when a man of such great influence made a commitment to the Lord, many others took note and became curious. In the first three years after his conversion, Jimmy was able to bring around two thousand to Christ. Each island had its own chief, so Jimmy concentrated on leading the chiefs to the Lord first. Across the hundreds of San Blas Islands, he became known as Brother Jimmy. When he died in a swimming accident in 1979 he left a tremendous legacy of mission work.

Dean remembers the last time he saw Jimmy. They chose a remote end of an island to talk, away from other people. Sitting together under the palm trees at sunset, Jimmy said, "Pray with me. We need some young men in the ministry here on the islands. Pray with me for guidance and direction from the Lord." Even as his last days were nearing, Brother Jimmy had a heart for the future of the island outreach. God knew that he would soon pass the baton to others.

We had the privilege of meeting Brother Jimmy. A simple fisherman who learned "sailor English" on a merchant ship, God blessed him and used him to bring the Gospel to the Cuna Indians. Upon meeting us, Jimmy invited us to share a meal with his family. His wife cooked over an open fire pit. He introduced us to his children and we worshiped with them and his friends and neighbors in their thatch-roofed church. What a privilege to know God was there, even on that remote Caribbean island.

Today many new young pastors and some strong older leaders work among the Cunas. The Indians still cling to their Cuna ways, but they know the Lord and follow God's teachings. When we look at what one man did among his neighbors, allowing himself to be used by God to change his small part of the world, we were motivated to continue seeking other places to do the same.

Flights to Colombia, Ecuador, Peru, Argentina, and Brazil further impacted our lives. In each country God had someone special—like Jimmy—for us to meet. The Lord prepared our path in amazing ways.

We were given the name of a Christian brother in Argentina, Andres Bokrand, from a German pastor in Nebraska. After arriving in Buenos Aires, we took the train and then a taxi to locate his house. We were surprised to find Andres standing in his front yard as though he waited for us during our entire eighteen-hour journey! He invited us inside and hurriedly brought in his relatives and friends to meet these strangers from North America.

Hospitality is very important in Latin America, and so the first order of business was to serve us their special form of hot tea, called *mate* (pronounced MAH-tay). This was our first encounter with their near-ceremonial method of drinking *mate*. One large silver cup with a strainer and a silver straw was passed to each person present. We tasted the hot sweet beverage and expressed our pleasure. While no one seemed to mind that we all used the same silver straw from a common cup, I was not accustomed to this. Being at the end of the line made my anxiousness grow. With nervous glances at each other, Chuck and I decided that the expression, "When in Rome, do as the Romans do," applied in this circumstance. There we were in communion with the people of God in Argentina; it was a privilege and we decided not to let our social norms get in the way of such special fellowship.

This kind of cultural and spiritual experience, with slight variations, happened in each of the countries we visited. The common love among God's people was producing a new dimension in our understanding of God's world.

Our continued search for God's plan found us journeying to the northern region of Argentina. We were to meet a Christian leader at Iguassu Falls, where Argentina, Paraguay, and Brazil come together. We boarded a commercial airline to Iguassu and were surprised when it landed on a grass strip in the middle of nowhere. There was no terminal, just a van that waited on the edge of the lonely field. As everyone began piling in, we crowded in, too.

The van took us to the Parana river, a huge, deep, fast-flowing body of water dividing the countries. We all got out and started down a steep path to a small boat dock. Now this was a little too much—no one told us about any river crossing! Chuck and I wondered if perhaps we boarded the wrong flight, or if some other misunderstanding occurred. We asked the van driver what was happening; where was the airplane terminal? Of course, we tried to ask all this with what little Spanish we knew.

One of the passengers coming out of the van overheard us struggling with the language, so he turned around and acted as our interpreter. He was able to explain that planes from Argentina were not allowed to fly to our destination in Brazil, the town of Iguassu. So the airplanes landed on the Argentinian side of the river, then ferried the passengers across the Parana to Brazil.

Okay, we thought, *if this is the way they do it, we'll do as the Romans do* again. However, I still asked, "What about the formalities, such as immigration and customs?"

"Oh, don't worry about that," they said, laughing. "There isn't anyone around here to check. We just go across the river and enter Brazil and that's that. If you don't come out of Brazil this way, you can always tell the authorities that you entered Brazil by the river crossing method, and they'll understand." We sure *hoped* we wouldn't get into any trouble with the immigration people in Brazil. In our country, the "river crossing method" is tantamount to illegal immigration! But we were flexible and went along with the program.

The "ferry" was really just a rowboat. It held four of us, along with our luggage, and thankfully made its way across each time with no problem. We were slightly nervous but the Lord was with us, and this trip was turning into more of an exciting adventure than we anticipated. Surely the Lord was leading us, because I don't think we could get in this kind of situation by ourselves!

Once across, we needed to find Tabitha Meiers, another woman whose name was given to us by the German pastor in

Nebraska. We wrote to her requesting to arrange a meeting in Iguassu but never heard back. Could we find her? A taxi-type vehicle was parked at the boat dock so we loaded our stuff and asked the driver to take us to a hotel. The best one was nearby the Falls, but when we checked inside, there wasn't anyone registered under Tabitha's name. The driver suggested the other hotel in the little town close by, so away we went. We decided en route that we would stay there whether or not Tabitha was around. Pulling our suitcases behind us in the dim light of evening, we headed to the hotel counter, when we heard our names called. It was Tabitha! She was sitting there in the lobby, waiting for us. What timing. What a miracle. What a Lord we have!

The next morning Tabitha took us by bus to the village of Rondon, some one hundred miles away. A camp meeting was underway when we arrived, but Tabitha and her mother told the people we were coming, so they were expecting us. They were mostly Germans who migrated to Brazil after World War II. The services were in German, the music included their German band, and the women cooked German food on a big stove outside in the courtyard. People had came from all over that area for the five-day meeting. Since none of them were used to seeing Americans in that part of Brazil, we were honored even though we felt like a curiosity.

They planned for Chuck to dedicate a church building for them in a neighboring village. What a privilege! In that simple building constructed with one-by-twelve-foot boards, and with only two kerosene lanterns illuminating the entire room, we joined with our new friends in praising God.

We went on from there to other Brazilian cities—Curitiba, Sao Paulo, and Rio de Janeiro before heading home. Although we saw many differences in the places we visited, we sensed a common connection. In each place a group of Christians loved the Lord and were committed to sharing the Gospel with their friends and neighbors so that others might come to know Jesus. And, most importantly, we were seeing ways we could help them do that very thing.

Stepping Forward

Returning home, we were changed people again. Our first journey to Mexico changed us, but God was after even more transformation in our minds and hearts. The Lord used these new experiences to continue opening our eyes and create in us a deepening desire to do more for him and for these Christian friends we found in each country.

Now came the questions: *What? How? Where? Who? Should we take the same kind of teams there that we took to Mexico?* We knew the bus couldn't drive as far as Argentina which is located nearly at the bottom of the world. The travel method we just used, flying, with the occasional river ferry—seemed to be the most logical, yet it seemed out of reach.

Chuck had his pilot's license for almost twenty years, but the planes he flew were small, two- or four-passenger models. *If we could only put wings on that bus, we thought, it would be perfect!* By now, we had paid the loan on the bus, so that freed up some resources, but it was only a beginning. Still, by faith we began to pray for an airplane, one big enough to carry all the people we traditionally transported by land.

In 1969, we thought first of a DC-3 model, since technology was not at the level of today's small-passenger planes. We found some for sale, but we weren't happy with them. Then Chuck heard of a forty-passenger plane, a twin-engine Convair in Dallas that was previously flown for Air Canada and more recently operated by Japan Air Lines. So Chuck headed for Dallas to check it out. Calling me excitedly one night, he said, "This is it! It'll do the job for us."

"Great news, Chuck. Let's take it," I said. We praised God together on the phone for leading us to the right plane. In all the excitement, though, I forgot to ask the price.

When Chuck returned, he brought a picture of the plane and information on its performance. He also had the price. I had to sit down. "Did you say *$35,000?* How can we ever handle that?" I was flabbergasted. The bus cost one-tenth of that, and we had thought *that* was a major mountain to climb.

It would have been easier to simply say no and go on with life. But life with the Lord is always an adventure in faith. Not always an easy one, true, but an enjoyable one if we let it be. Trusting God, means trusting God with each step of the journey. We had a burning desire to get people to these new mission fields. So we prayed. Then we stepped forward.

A Leap of Faith

We decided to buy the plane. I call this kind of action "faith risk." I call it risk because it's not the same as gambling or reckless behavior, even though some folks who don't understand walking with our adventuresome God might view it that way. Rather, it's taking baby steps of faith, pushing us to the edges of our comfort zones. It's sort of a spiritual version of the old expression, "Nothing ventured, nothing gained." With God on our side, it's not as risky as it feels. And the benefits are very great.

Obviously we had to raise the money to pay for it. And since it wasn't a new plane, a great deal of maintenance was needed. Plus, Chuck was not licensed to fly anything that big, so he had to receive additional flight instruction and get "type-rated" on a Convair.

This was July 1969. We planned to take our first trip to Panama in November. That gave us a little more than three months to raise the money, get the plane airworthy, get Chuck's type-rating, find the rest of the crew (we needed an additional type-rated co-pilot and a stewardess), make the arrangements for the first trip, and find forty people who wanted to go.

We wondered at times, *Are we up to climbing this mountain?* Of course, we were still pastoring the church, which was experiencing a growth spurt. We certainly never attempted anything such as this before. But this is what we felt the Lord would have us do.

Chuck spent a great deal of his time in Dallas preparing the plane and working on his type rating. The aircraft was being prepped by some Delta Airlines mechanics, and if they said the plane needed a certain part, Chuck told them to get it. New tires? No problem. Additional radios? Go buy them. His purpose was to get the plane in tip-top shape. We were going to put forty passengers in that plane (plus the crew), and we didn't want any mistakes.

Back in Wichita we started raising the funds. We went to our relatives and friends for help. They were encouraging and made donations—one as large as $3,000. We were getting there, but not quite enough to cover all the costs.

Getting the type rating was expensive, too. Chuck needed an instructor, and naturally he had to fuel the plane as he practiced. Plus there was the cost of transportation to and from Dallas. Because of these expenses, Chuck slept in the plane or on the ground under it when he was in Dallas. Anything to cut costs.

I prepared information on the trip to Panama and, sure enough, people responded. Participants came from Illinois, Missouri, and Oklahoma as well as Kansas. They were sending their money ($290 per person for all expenses on the trip) and planning to arrive on Tuesday night as we were scheduled to depart on Wednesday morning.

Chuck kept the checkbook while he stayed in Dallas, and when he came home two weeks before our departure, he asked me to bring it up to date. What a shock. With what he spent and what we needed in our pockets to take with us on the trip, we were $10,000 short. That was as much as our salary for a year!

We had to do something. First, I went to the bank and talked to the president, Bob McGrath. He was sympathetic and said we could work something out. Then we put together a proposal that Chuck would take to some doctors and other professionals to raise $10,000. We had just two weeks to find $10,000. The first week Chuck spent talking to potential donors. They told him they needed to talk to their wives or their CPAs and he could get back with them the following week.

When he returned the second week, they had either "gone fishing," forgotten all about it, or gave a negative response. It was the weekend before our Wednesday departure. That weekend we prayed more than usual and decided we would work on it Monday. When Monday morning came we pulled out our notes, although they were engraved on our minds, to see whom we had yet to approach.

The first call was to a doctor whom we had never met, Dr. Thompson. Chuck talked to his wife and she said that they *did* plan to help us. We sensed a miracle coming. As Chuck got around to asking how much they might give, she said, "Would $10,000 help?" Praise God! Now the Lord was supplying it all at one time. Chuck continued the conversation to find out when he could pick up the donation. She said that he could come by the office on Tuesday at 2:00 P.M. This was one day before we were scheduled for departure to Panama with forty people. You can bet Chuck was on time for that exchange!

Walking in the bank that afternoon, I was a bit fearful that we were overdrawn and the bank president had forgotten to call me. Talking first to his secretary, I inquired if he was in the office. Then he saw me and stepped through his doorway to say, "You told me that you wrote a lot of checks and could be overdrawn. Nothing has come in yet."

Amazing. How strange. I could hardly believe it; those checks were written more than two weeks prior. Then I saw Chuck walking in the bank door. I rushed over to tell him the news and to see if he had the check for $10,000. He did. What a blessing.

It was 3:00 P.M and the funds we needed for the trip were in our pockets. People were already arriving. God supplied the funds just in time, through one of his servants.

The next morning we all boarded the plane, and what a group! These people came with great expectations and excitement to join our first eyewitness crusade. More than half of them were first-time flyers, so it was an additional new experience for them. We left Wichita at 5:00 A.M.

Our first stop was in Dallas to pick up the life jackets and rafts we needed. That took a while. Next we stopped in Galveston, Texas, to refuel before heading across the Gulf of Mexico. The persons at the fueling station were expecting us but weren't expecting a plane as big as ours. Those reciprocal engines on the Convair used lots of oil. Refueling didn't take long if they supplied it by the gallons, but in Galveston they only had quarts. This took ninety minutes more than we planned. Our "over-water" segment of the flight went well, and our next stop was Merida, Mexico, for more fuel. Our route then took us toward the Swan Islands, across the Caribbean to San Andres Island for our last fuel stop before arriving in Panama.

With the stop for the life rafts and the fueling delay in Galveston, we were running late. As we radioed our position to the Swan Islands, they told us that there was a storm ahead but it shouldn't be a bother to us. We headed south, and because of our delay it was now getting dark. The storm caused our plane to start bouncing around a bit. Our first-time flyers began to get frightened because of the turbulence. My job was to keep everybody comfortable; I was the stewardess, having taken training on emergency procedures before we left. This was certainly not a job that my role as pastor's wife prepared me for. *How can I calm their fears?* I thought.

I remembered that I experienced a greater fear two weeks before, when we didn't have the $10,000 we needed. Since God took care of us then, God surely could take care of us now. It was time to tell them about the $10,000 miracle. So I related the story of how the Lord supplied the plane in the first place, how we—by faith—got it airworthy, how we were short $10,000, and how just yesterday the Lord gave us this miracle and supplied the funds while they were arriving. The God who gave us $10,000 one day was not going to fail us the next day. He wasn't going to abandon us over the Caribbean Sea.

Shortly after that story, we started our descent. And as we came out from under those dark clouds, we saw the landing strip on San Andres Island—right in front of us. The God of miracles wants us to trust him, to move on in spite of our mistakes and fears that arise while walking the road God prepares for us. No, God doesn't write us letters telling us all about this adventure with him, but God did place in writing many years ago these beautiful words: "Never will I leave you; / never will I forsake you" (Heb 13:5, NIV).

Flying through the air to a strange island country, running out of daylight and having just skirted a bucking bronco of a thunderstorm, it was back to basics—faith and trust. God didn't lead us down that path to harm us, but rather, God had his plans for us. Our part was simply to, as the Scriptures say, "Trust in the LORD with all your heart / and lean not on your own understanding; / in all your ways acknowledge him, / and he will make your paths straight" (Prov 3:5–6, NIV).

Seems like faith and money, or the lack of it, often go together. The fact that the Lord supplied the $10,000 is bottom-line evidence that we were doing what God planned for us. That's the kind of confirmation we all need.

I often wonder what would have happened if we chose not to take that faith risk but backed off from the plans God had in mind. Without the faith and obedience in taking that first trip to Mexico in our little family car, there might not have been a bus; without the bus, more than half of our congregation wouldn't have been exposed to Mexican missions, and there might not have been an airplane and all the growth that followed for our missions ministry, Project Partner.

With that airplane we took more than 6,000 people to the Caribbean, Central America, and South America over ten years.

Hundreds of churches, schools, clinics, and parsonages were constructed because of these trips—even a hangar for Christian pilots in Guatemala.

Looking back we see how the Lord led us. This gives us faith to take the next step and say, "Yes, Lord." It is challenging and exhilarating. It makes us ready to climb the next mountain even though it looks much different—and sometimes more difficult—than the one we just mastered. But God provides the grace to ascend each peak, if we will trust him.

CHAPTER 3
ADVENTURE: IF ONE DOOR IS CLOSED,
FIND ANOTHER

Meeting Challenges

What do you do if the door is shut? Somewhere in our spiritual journey that began by starting a church in 1952 and led to developing the ministry of Project Partner, the Lord showed Chuck and me the principle of finding a way to accomplish the vision. It's that "one step at a time" principle. When you find a closed door, you don't give up; you search for another way to achieve your goal. You don't give in to adversity, you use it as a challenge to find another way.

I think this goes back to the principle that the Lord illustrated with Joseph, recounted in Genesis 50:20. Things often intended to harm us or to stop us can be used by the Lord to put us on the track that he wanted us on in the first place. God uses it for our good. Such was the case after we bought the airplane and wanted to work extensively with our denomination.

Before we purchased the plane in 1969 and while it was still a dream, Chuck went to the missions agency of the Church of God to get their stamp of approval. He wanted to help them. Chuck felt we could get more people interested in missions if they traveled to those mission fields and saw the needs for themselves. We could show them the people, the native pastors, the missionaries, and what the Lord was doing among them. That's what happened to our family. Chuck thought he had the approval of the missions agency to proceed.

After we bought the plane, however, the agency appeared to rethink this situation. This was not the way missions was handled in those days. They anticipated too much risk with liability. They also told us it would be better not to use their name or refer to them in any way. This was not what we wanted or needed. We wanted to help them, but it was evident that it was not to be accepted that way.

So what was our alternative? We could sell the plane and forget the whole idea or we could find another way to make it work. We chose the latter wondering what "another way" would be. Up to that time, everything we had done and all we knew was the Church of God (Anderson, Indiana). Chuck grew up in the Church of God in Dayton, Ohio, and I had the heritage of my grandmother helping start the Church of God in Tulsa, Oklahoma. We had met at Anderson College, a Church of God affiliated school. We went from college to take a position as associate pastor with E. E. Kardatzke at the First Church of God in Wichita, Kansas. Then we started the Pawnee Avenue Church of God, and by the time we bought the plane we had pastored it for eighteen years. All we knew was the Church of God and we loved it.

Now we had our dream and we also had a problem. We went to our attorney friend, Justus Fugate, and incorporated our dream in the fall of 1968. In the process Justus asked Chuck what he wanted to name this corporation. We never discussed this so it was a surprise to me when Chuck thought a minute and came up with Project Partner. This dear attorney helped us put together a nonprofit corporation and get the IRS approval for our 501 (c) 3 tax status. He was always there to help us and told Chuck many times that his purpose was to keep Chuck out of trouble.

Our first trip with the plane was that one to Panama in November 1969. Taking people on the bus for five years helped us develop a small mailing list and somewhat of a reputation. It wasn't too hard to fill up the plane for that first flight since what we were doing was unique and caught people's interest.

The hard part was figuring what the cost per passenger would be each trip. We never knew how many people we would have, so to divide the expense of fuel, flight service, pilot fees, and other expenses into an unknown number of passengers made every trip a financial gamble. We also covered the maintenance costs, and in aviation that can be quite high. You have to have an A&P licensed mechanic to work on a plane, a commercial type rating to fly it, and training to be a stewardess. Those were additional costs. Plus, we worried about where to park it and how much that would cost. Airplanes were different than buses. We had to fly it regularly, at least once a week, to keep everything working and functioning properly. Those trips cost money. No, let me rephrase that, planes cost money.

Chuck completed his type rating as captain. We encouraged Harold Perry and Loren Ralston from our church to earn their licenses so they could fly with him. Joe Hooker, a pilot during World War II, already had his type rating, and was available to go with us although he pastored a church in Oklahoma. We hired a mechanic. There were numerous people in our church who helped us with cleaning the plane and caring for it.

Our first workcamp came about with a group from Indianapolis in January of 1970. They came with a leader so our job was simply to get the group to Panama and back. That being the case, we decided to take our three boys with us enabling us to have a vacation while the Indy team was building a church near Colon.

Still, the problem with the missions agency remained. We wanted to help them but they didn't want anything to do with us. If we were going to develop our missions outreach we needed to find some way to reach churches and get them interested in this new kind of ministry. We also had to keep the plane flying.

One method we dreamed up: enlisting people from our congregation to fly the forty or so miles with us from Wichita to Hutchinson, Kansas, for Sunday dinner at the nice airport restaurant. That thirty-minute flight each way kept the plane active, the passengers paid enough to cover the cost of the gasoline, and we made a great excursion out of it. This worked for about a year as our monthly dinner flight.

After our first workcamp trip, we began developing the workcamp program. This new idea immediately caught the attention of people who wanted to "do something" for missions. We discovered, however, because we were not limited to Church of God that we should reach out to other churches and groups.

Obviously you start where you are, so we started in Wichita with pastors that Chuck met during the previous twenty years. It wasn't long before we were taking the First Evangelical Free Church to Mexico to build a church. We transported University Baptist and Immanuel Baptist to work in Central America. Central Christian Church loaded the plane with its people for a trip to Guatemala.

Then came the earthquake in Nicaragua in 1972. We enlisted people from every church we could to go with us to help at that time of need and reconstruction. Taking a reporter from the Wichita newspaper with us gave us press coverage that enabled us to reach out to more churches in Kansas.

We found workers from the Christian churches, the Methodist churches, the Presbyterian churches, Mennonite, and many others. It was exciting to meet these people and work with them. They were open, they wanted to help, and they would assist us locating others to get involved. It was also God's way of expanding our vision and developing relationships across denominational lines.

In 1975 the General Assembly of the Church of God chose to recognize Project Partner as a para-mission group, giving us status in working with the Church of God. Prior to this they conducted several meetings—difficult meetings—with us. They wanted to know more about what we were doing; they wanted to *control* our activities. Fortunately, the action of the General Assembly did not restrict us at all, rather they gave us a position of affiliation with the church. By now, we had our own vision of expanding the Kingdom of God and were thoroughly enjoying working with other churches with their own visions for the world.

We were taking teams from Indianapolis, Louisville, Birmingham, Phoenix, St. Louis, Chicago, Akron, Denver, Houston, Minneapolis, Lexington, Tulsa, Kansas City, Dayton,

Morehead, Youngstown, Fort Wayne, Marion, Illinois; Washington, DC, and Detroit. But more importantly, the Lord opened a new door for us: working with many evangelical churches across the United States. What was meant to restrain us was used for good. Our vision of the Kingdom of God and the oneness of God's people was now etched in our minds.

The message of Jesus Christ is always the same. It never changes. But the methods to share it change continually. What works one time doesn't work the next time. What is the best way at one time is hampered by tradition through the years. As one door is closed, it doesn't mean that we are to quit. It means we find another way, another door.

We were the forerunners of workcamps in the early 1970s. They were great. They did a tremendous amount of good for the Christians in those many countries including Peru, Panama, Barbados, El Salvador, Honduras, Belize, Haiti, Grenada, Trinidad, Nicaragua, Guatemala, and Mexico. We are proud of those years and those accomplishments. They enabled the local churches to take giant steps in reaching their people for Christ.

Flying our airplane was spectacular. It certainly got people's attention. Then came another fuel crunch and deregulation. A door was closing. It was time to find another way. There was a time to fight the system and there was a time to recognize the difficulties and look for another way.

The "system" was always a problem. This "system" I am referring to is the regulatory agencies that governed flying a forty-passenger plane. When we bought our first plane we had the Civil Aviation Board (CAB), the Federal Aviation Authority (FAA), the Treasury Department, and Immigration and Customs to deal with.

Back in 1969 any commercial airline was assigned air routes by the CAB. Airlines could not simply choose where they wanted to fly nor how often. Chuck went to Washington to see where we would be able to fly our plane. When they heard that he wanted to pick up passengers in Indianapolis or St. Louis or Birmingham, or wherever and whenever we had a workcamp project scheduled, they actually laughed at him. That wasn't possible. We had to find another way.

Because Wichita was the center of aviation at that time for Boeing, Cessna, Beech, and Lear Aircraft factories, we were able to find a good attorney who understood the problem. He and Chuck worked together and found the way to fly within the CAB's Part 91 stipulation, which was basically a club arrangement. Everyone who wanted to go with us joined "the club" and simply paid a share of expenses. And it worked. We found a way to fly our plane for mission trips. We presented our method to the CAB and they agreed that it would work.

We located a young pilot named Don Shaver at Gulf Coast Bible College in Houston with a commercial and instrument license and he was ready to work for Ozark Airlines. When we presented our project to Don, he chose to come fly for us. Don and Chuck made a good team pouring over the FAA books to see how we could comply with all the demands and requirements. They wrote manuals concerning maintenance and procedures. Whatever the FAA required, they found a way to satisfy it. But it was not without cost or problems. There was even one FAA man in Kansas City that told Chuck he didn't want us to fly and would see to it that we were grounded someday, some way. Fortunately, he didn't succeed, although he was always there monitoring our activities.

Then there was the Treasury Department and Immigration and Customs. They had never regulated a plane like ours either so they didn't quite know how to handle us when we left and reentered the United States. We finally obtained an exemption status since we qualified as a "charitable and religious organization." We could enter the country with only a minimum fee instead of the tremendous fees that commercial carriers have to pay.

These were obstacles to be overcome on a continual basis. But with the help of the Lord we were able to fly our planes, the Convair first and later the Fairchild 27, from 1969 to 1977. In 1977 we changed our methods and sold the F27. Keeping a forty-passenger plane in the air, making it safe for our people, dealing with the government agencies, and obtaining permits in foreign countries for refueling as well as all the entry requirements were always major tasks. I remember going to see the movie *Airport* in 1971. In that story there were so many employees with their assigned jobs. Chuck and I just laughed as we realized that between the two of us and a couple of people to help us, we did all of those jobs ourselves.

It wasn't always that way though. Soon we had people coming to help us. There were Dick and Fran Sanders in Marion, Illinois. He flew for TWA as well as the Air National Guard. They moved to Wichita to help us. Dick was a great pilot and Fran helped as a stewardess when their two little boys were able to go along.

There were Claude and Jan Ferguson from Alliance, Ohio. They caught the vision knowing that with his skills in construction, Claude could handle the workcamp department. They, with their four children, packed up and moved to Wichita.

John and Betty Wren felt the Lord calling them to come help and left Birmingham, Alabama, to join the team. Following them were Chester and Patsy Lemmond from Alabama, the Reverend Jim and Lois Comstock from Illinois, the Reverend Dan and Betty Ann Harman from Kentucky, Brenda Barlow from Louisiana, the Reverend Gayle and Alice Van Asdale from Missouri, Joy Wharton and David Massey from Ohio, Greg and Gail Bratton along with Ricka Brady and Faith King from Indiana, and Norm Carr, Jeanne Cornelius, Chuck and Shirley Moore, David and Judy Lymer, Gene and Ruth Basquez, Milton and Norma Regnier, Harold Perry, Eric Bergquist, and Loren and Lemoine Ralston. They all left their jobs and came to work with us because they believed in this ministry. And there were more. We had quite a team.

We surely needed them, but how did we get so many? The Lord called them and they raised their own support and came by faith. They were modern day Abrahams who were willing to leave their homeland, and go into a land they did not know in order to be obedient to the Lord's call upon their life. This was adventure for them. It was also obedience to the call of God. Since there weren't funds for their support, they found another way—they were willing and able to raise support from their home church, relatives, and friends so that they could do the Lord's work. They found a way. They chose adventure with God. And they got it.

Don't Rock the Boat

I guess anything can be an adventure if you haven't done it before and everything is so totally different. That very first trip we took to Panama, the one when the Lord provided a $10,000 miracle and we flew through the storm over the Caribbean to get there, was an adventure.

Dean Flora, the missionary, was showing us around Panama. We were an eager bunch wanting to see everything. The canal and the enormous ships going through that narrow waterway held our attention. The difference between the Canal Zone controlled by the United States and the rest of Panama showed us the stark contrast between their culture and ours, as well as the economic differences. But Dean wanted us to see more.

He took us to the churches in the Panama City area and we thoroughly enjoyed that experience. He opened up his home and invited Mendoza and Daisy Taylor, Francisco Pitty, and other national leaders for us to meet them. The church in Colon on the Caribbean side held a special service for us. Leaving the church, Dean pulled Chuck aside and said, "Chuck, I have another church I think you would like to visit. It isn't so easy to get to. In fact, we will have to go up a river in the jungle in canoes. But you would really like it and they would certainly welcome you. It is a lot different but these people know the Lord and I think this would be good for your group and good for those Indian people in that church, too. What do you think?"

Dean knew that Chuck liked challenges so he wasn't at all surprised when Chuck answered yes. This would be even more exciting and different from anything we ever imagined before.

The next morning we got an early start piling onto a bus and heading on up the coast from Colon. This meant we got to drive over the Panama Canal truck bridge, past the American military base, and through some five Indian villages until we came to the mouth of the Rio Indio. Bus rides were normal, but things soon became very different.

Our group divided up and climbed into numerous canoes for the hour-long trip up the river. Apprehensively Chuck looked at the forty people in the *cayucas* canoes. *"What am I doing?"* he thought to himself. *"I'll be lucky if fifteen of them don't drown and the rest of us are not eaten by alligators."* Aloud he said, "Sit still, folks, don't rock the boat. There are no life jackets so you won't have a second chance here."

The water of the Rio Indio rode high on the cayucas, threatening to spill into the boat at the slightest movement. The extreme heat and humidity made everyone uncomfortable and, in other circumstances, the river water might have seemed a welcomed relief. But there was nothing welcoming in the Rio Indio, she was filled with huge alligators.

Panama seemed the perfect place for the Convair, our first airplane, to take the first EyeWitness Crusade group. It was far enough away to be a good experience. In Dean Flora they would see a missionary dedicated to his people, one who knew how to use the many seemingly useless resources available in this area for the cause of Christ. Among other things, he taught his young people how to use a broken pop bottle to scrape out pieces of wood and make bowls to sell.

Chuck intended for the tour group to have a jungle trip and see the jungle tone, but as he looked at their anxious faces and white knuckles, he wasn't so sure he meant for them to see this much.

Dean made all the arrangements for the trip and was accompanying us on this journey up the Rio Indio. When we finally pulled to shore, he led us down the path to a small church made of vertical sticks tied together. Inside there was barely enough room for the forty of us to perch on the boards meant for benches.

Unusual sounds filled the air—monkeys chattering, birds calling. The heat was most oppressive, plus everyone soon discovered sand fleas. Cautiously we were joined by the local Christians, led by Pastor Dionecio. Small, dark, barefoot Indian people with questioning eyes peered from the jungle foliage. Never in their lives had they seen a group like this.

Chuck was warned to leave there well before dark. We could not navigate our way back without lights and we didn't have any. Following a short service with the congregation singing for us and with the pastor giving us words of welcome, we prepared to leave. Then O. C. Lewis, a member of our group, suggested that we take a small offering for our new friends, these Indian Christian brothers and sisters. Of course, we all liked that idea. Chuck took off his straw hat and it was quickly passed among our group. It was piled pretty high with dollar bills when it came back to Chuck and he handed it to Pastor Dionecio. Dean helped him count it and it amounted to one hundred and ten dollars. Dean suggested they should pray and Pastor Dionecio began. It soon became apparent that the pastor was very emotionally repeating the same phrase over and over.

"What's going on?" Chuck whispered to Dean.

"Sh-h-h-h."

At the conclusion of the prayer, Dean turned toward us. "Perhaps," he said, "I should explain to you what happened here. You see, these people have never seen that much money before." Then turning to Chuck he said, "Chuck, I've been in your church in Wichita; how much would you say it is worth?"

"Oh, $500,000, I suppose," Chuck answered.

"Right. Suppose that next Sunday a group of Indians came to your church and at the close of the service they take up an offering and hand it to you. Now, just what would your prayer be if the amount were to be $500,000?

"You see, you have just given these people the equivalent of this property and this building. They are overwhelmed. When Pastor Dionecio tried to pray, all he could say was, 'Thank you, Jesus. Thank you, Jesus. Thank you, Jesus.' "

Slowly a fear crept into Chuck as he listened to Dean speak. He knew that money, a lot of money, has the potential to harm rather than help, and Chuck was afraid of what our group might have done to this small jungle congregation.

"Oh, Dean, have we done wrong?"

"I have confidence in my people, in God's people," Dean said.

"But what will they do with that much money? How will they handle it?" Chuck asked, concern in his voice.

"Let's ask them," Dean suggested.

Pastor Dionecio listened quietly to the question put to him. Finally he spoke.

"We have discussed it," he said slowly and deliberately, "and we have decided. We are so fortunate. We know the Lord Jesus. Up the river they do not know him. They need to know. They need a church. We will go up the river and build a church."

CHAPTER 4

SERVANTHOOD: BEING THE CONDUIT

Although we visited Mexico many times, we had never heard of the Zoque Indians. Then Ed Aulie showed up. Ed was a missionary down in the state of Chiapas, Mexico, among the Zoque. He made the long trip to Wichita to see us and enlist our help. But Ed wasn't asking for a church building, although they really needed one. What Ed was asking for was a water system.

"Ed," Chuck responded, "we don't do water systems. We help by building churches or clinics or schools."

"Is it not true that your purpose is to help the people in the greatest way possible to the glory of God? Is this not true?" Ed asked.

"Yes, it is true," Chuck replied.

"Chuck and Donna, the Zoque people, for the most part, have nothing to do with churches. Their greatest need is for water. It takes water to live. If we could show them that because we are Christians, we are concerned about helping them to have water, it would be a most effective witness."

"So," Chuck said slowly, "you want us to help build you a water system?"

"Oh, yes, please. They need one so badly. In the rainy season there is water everywhere. At that time there is too much water, but it doesn't last long and then the dry season sets in. Each time the dry season seems to last longer than the time before, and you find yourself beginning to fear that by the time it is over practically everything will have died."

Their Needs or Ours

Chuck was thinking of what we always did in the past. When we started taking teams to build churches in Guatemala or Nicaragua, our men looked at the way the Nicaraguans or Guatemalans constructed their buildings and immediately set out to show them a better way, the American way. Only one problem: the local people didn't want it that way. So were we going to build an American building or a Guatemalan building? Who was going to use it and what did *they* want? Would we build their way but grumble all the time? Were we there to be served or to serve?

We knew that we were to take teams to different countries and build church buildings for the native people. We thought we were really good at it. We built more than thirty churches in Guatemala alone, plus those we built in the other Latin American countries with our workcamp teams. We became well-known, and various groups and missionaries were asking for our help. It was exciting.

Ed went on, "These people need help. Water is the priority. It is an urgent need for them."

"Is there no source of water, other than rainfall, that you can tap into?" Chuck questioned.

"Well, yes. High up in the mountains there are springs."

"It seems that the best way to help you and your people is to harness the springs and build a reservoir." Chuck was thinking out loud about the problem, and he recognized the difficulty of the rugged terrain. "This will take an especially hardy group of workcampers. But I think we have just the right leader for this, Milton Regnier. Yes, Ed, we'll work with you and find a group that wants an especially challenging job. We'll ask Milton to lead it."

We did find a group. The First Evangelical Free Church in Wichita was ready to meet this challenge. They found the workers. We made arrangements for the workcampers to fly into Mexico via Mexican Airlines. The next leg of the trip was with Missionary Aviation Fellowship, who flew them by groups of three into a jungle strip aboard their Cessna 185 plane. From there they left behind all known modes of travel. The rest of the journey was ten long miles up the trail into the steep mountains by mule.

The Zoque Indians surely never saw anything to equal the arrival of thirty white North Americans on muleback, packing a tremendous yardage of white plastic pipe and numerous bags filled with cement.

Knowing that there would not be sufficient food for the workers—the Indians barely had enough for themselves—it was also Milton's responsibility to arrange for the workers to bring with them enough food to sustain them during the time they would be isolated in the mountains.

Here was a true test of servanthood for this team. No amount of telling the team what they would find or where they were going could have prepared them for the realities that they encountered. How could they understand that their home for those two weeks would be a bamboo hut? It would appear to be a scene straight out of *National Geographic*.

This workcamp involved digging ditches, laying pipe, mixing cement, moving rocks, carrying supplies, preparing food outdoors, and washing clothes by hand—really hard work. And it all had to be accomplished with a cheerful attitude and a smile. They put Matthew 25:35 into action "I was thirsty and you gave me something to drink."

The challenge of the Zoque Indians' need brought Chuck and me to the understanding that we were to be their servants, work with them, help them, support them, do it their way, and let them determine what was best for *their* people and *their* country.

This thing of servanthood doesn't come naturally—and it seems harder for Americans. We often feel that we have all the answers and all other cultures and ways of doing things simply don't live up to what we can do.

Before this trip I previously bought into the concept that we in the West are to be the missionaries, go to a foreign field, develop a church, and see to it that everything is done *correctly*. There certainly was a time when that was right, but that was before we started taking so many people to these foreign fields. A new understanding of a people's right to their own culture replaced the idea the "natives" had to follow our culture.

In the beginning of modern missions in the 1800s and 1900s, missionaries went to these foreign fields. They led native people to Christ and they identified and trained Christian leaders. Now, however, our role as American missionaries changed. To be the most effective, to do the most for the Lord, and to reach the most people for Christ, we were learning that the *national* workers could do the best job. They certainly knew the culture, the language, and they understood the "systems," plus they didn't need a visa to get into their country or to stay there. And they were there for life. No furloughs were necessary. They were the front line for Christ.

We were also learning at this time that we had a different responsibility. I discovered my role was to be the partner and the conduit with productive national leaders. I was to enable them to develop, enhance, and expand the work of the Lord in their country.

The Zoque Indians were tremendously pleased with the water system our team of North Americans provided. Each evening they showed up as the team ended the day with a worship service. They wanted to know more about these strange white people. The Zoques listened to the message of Jesus Christ, discovering that Jesus was the one who made these strangers different and willing to serve them. Ed Aulie told us later that this was a turning point in their acceptance of the Gospel.

God Changes Our Course

While riding a train in India and listening to the wheels bounce over the rails, I was in deep thought. *What would the Lord want us to do here? What would be most productive for the Kingdom?* I realized I needed to change the ministry of Project

Partner and focus on national leaders. Seems like the Lord used trips to get my attention and to help me see the direction he wanted me to go. That day in January 1987, bumping along those rails, among so many Indian people with all their complexities, the realization came that the Lord had put tremendous national leaders in my path for a reason. He wanted me to serve them by getting American Christians involved in the leaders' existing ministries. The native Christian leaders I'd been meeting and working with over the last several years were reaching thousands of their own people for the Lord in ways no American ever could. The best thing I could do to help them was to serve them. I could bring them to the United States once or twice a year, get them into our churches to meet people, and find partners for them to develop their ministry further.

Since I was already in India, I presented this idea to the Reverend Samuel Stephens and his father, the Reverend Raja Stephens, president of the India Gospel League. They were ready. I first met Samuel when he showed up at the Project Partner office in October 1984. There he was, a young man direct from India wanting to talk with me. He rather nervously showed me pictures of the India Gospel League's work in India. These photos were black and white, not too impressive, but his sincerity and earnestness were impressive. He really came to ask me to provide $4,500 to build a church in India.

"Samuel," I stated, "This looks very good, but I really don't know you and we don't have money for your project at this time."

His countenance fell, but he was not ready to give up. "I would like to show you some pictures of our children. We have 800 orphan children that we are taking care of and there are thousands more that are waiting for help. We bring these children into our facility and provide housing, medical care, good nutrition, education, and of course, Christian training. Would it be possible to provide support for some children? There are so very many that are in urgent need of help. A lot of them are street children or from families so poor that they cannot care for them."

I was thinking, *We already have a children's program, our Agape program. We are providing sponsors for children in Guatemala, Nicaragua, Costa Rica, Panama, Haiti, and El Salvador. Maybe we could help some here. That is, if he could provide us with good references.*

"Samuel," I responded, "we could probably help you with your children's program if you could send me some references as to the work of the India Gospel League. Would you get me a letter of reference from the president of the Evangelical Association of Asia, the Reverend Theodore Williams, and also one from the president of the Evangelical Association of India, the Reverend John Richard?"

Samuel left that day assuring me that he would provide the letters. So I assured him that we would start sponsoring some of his children as soon as we received that endorsement. In a few months the letters were on my desk. The idea of serving national leaders was still in the back of my mind.

By 1986 we were sponsoring nearly fifty children for Samuel when he called from Portland, Oregon. He was back in the United States searching for funding, and he wanted to come see me. This time he was at our office on a Tuesday when we held our weekly chapel service for the staff, so I asked him to share his pictures and ministry with all of us. This time he had slides, and as he was showing them and explaining each picture, my heart was responding to the work in India. I felt that this young man was one we needed to work with in a much greater degree than just the children's program.

In the fall of 1988 I brought him to the United States so that we could work together to find partners for his ministry. I was to make the appointments that would put him into meetings and churches that might be interested in supporting him. We learned a lot about each other in those six weeks. We drove my car more than 3,500 miles around Ohio, Kentucky, Tennessee, Indiana, and Illinois. We also traveled by air to Seattle.

Bringing Samuel into our house and our lives was exactly what Chuck and I wanted. He was about the age of our oldest son, and having just lost his father that spring, Samuel accepted Chuck's offer to be his father now. That relationship became very precious to him and to us. Years earlier we had learned from Enrique Cepeda, the Spanish expression, *"Me casa es su casa"* or "My house is your house." It is a joy and privilege to provide a home for Samuel when he comes to the United States.

Although Samuel was very attuned to American culture, it became my role to serve him by helping him to continue to learn our ways. Samuel was an excellent driver in India, which is a tremendous challenge. There you drive defensively at all times. You have to have eyes in the back of your head, be willing to be challenged, and give in easily to the bigger vehicle. It is obvious that the biggest bus or truck wins, and if you weren't driving the biggest vehicle, you had better get out of the way. As he faced the challenges of our interstate highway system, Samuel soon learned they were not the same. He discovered that you don't wait for everyone to get out of your way to get on to the Interstate here. He quickly learned when I encouraged him, or should we say yelled to him, "Go, go, go!"

Like Samuel, Enrique needed the same kind of help. Getting both of them driver's licenses was interesting, too. They took the written and driving tests. This was a challenge for them, but they made it fine. The biggest hurdle was probably helping the clerk understand that they didn't have United States social security numbers.

Banking in India is usually a half-day affair. I thoroughly enjoyed showing them our drive-in facilities and the ATM machine. They couldn't believe you could do bank business so fast. You didn't have to wait until the clerk found the right ledger book, carried it in, found the page with your account, and then wrote down your transaction. They couldn't believe either that you could write everything out once and be done with it.

During the next few months, I brought each of the nationals we were working with at that time—Lener Cauper and Salomon Cabanillas from Peru, Joe Surin from Haiti, Pastor

Loo from China, Guillermo Villanueva and Enrique Cepeda from Mexico, Ali Velasquez from Nicaragua, and Samuel Stephens from India—to the States for itineration. My new goal was to help them enlist partners for their ministry.

As I began to serve these men in the new way God was showing me, I began to see how much the church in America needs them in order to be obedient to the Great Commission. My role was to put these men and the people of the American church together. We worked out an agreement between our national leaders. They would be in charge of what happened in their country. I would be in charge of what happened in the States. We would help them and be available to them as needed. All of the funds we raised were to go through Project Partner, providing financial accountability for them. Regular financial reports were to be sent to our office. They were to come to the States at least once a year for itineration or to visit their partners. I, or a delegate, was to go to their country at least once a year to see what was going on and be an encouragement.

It became apparent to me that one way they needed to be served was by helping their wives know what was occurring. Another mountain. Could we possibly get them all together for a week? We could call it a congress and let the leaders meet each other, learn from each other, pray together, develop relationships, and bring their wives with them so that their families would understand better their growing work in the States. Talk about a mountain, this was a steep one. The biggest obstacle was finding money. There were airfares for two, the language problem with the China pastor, working out time commitments, finding a place where everyone could stay for a week, putting together a program that would benefit them, and providing some new contacts since they were already in the States.

The decision to have this congress had to be made a minimum of nine months ahead. Remember "faith risk"? This was certainly one of those times. But one night as I was wrestling with this, I felt the Lord saying, "Trust me." "Okay, Lord, are you talking about the congress or something else? The way things are right now, the office needs your help too." He meant the congress. Within a couple of days I decided to go for it. So we took the first step, found the next one, moved up the mountain, and in October 1989 we brought all the national leaders and their wives together for a great and wonderful week of training and new connections for their national ministries.

A retreat center near Cincinnati, Ohio, was the perfect place. We provided the format for the congress and the first day's agenda, and then we turned it over to the national leaders for their own ideas and leadership to surface. It was a great time for them, a refreshing of their spirit, a building of their faith, a special communion. Climaxing that week, Dr. Milton Grannum, pastor in Philadelphia but a native of Guyana, came to lead them into a greater challenge for the future and the assurance that we were here to serve them, to assist them, and to be their partners in ministry. This was indeed a mountaintop experience, a time of unity, purpose, commitment, challenge, and building lasting relationships. Mountaintops are wonderful because you have reached a goal and the view from the top is always spectacular and far-reaching.

Serving the Pastors

Another very productive way I previously found to serve national leaders was to provide leadership teams to train groups of native pastors. This idea came as I was in Peru. The pastors seemed to have a tremendous dedication. Their spirit seemed so genuine. How did they become pastors? Several told me how the Lord called them to serve. One was in jail and an evangelist came there to preach. He accepted the Lord and promised that when he was freed, he would serve the Lord. Others had unique stories of the Lord calling them as well.

I inquired as to where these pastors were trained. The answer was always that they didn't have any training. It simply wasn't available. These pastors were totally on their own. My next question was what books or resources they used to help them in their ministry. The answer: We have our Bible but nothing else. I felt something had to be done. Surely I could help them. I scheduled the first training experience for Lima, Peru, in 1983. I wanted to try it and see if it would meet their needs.

Two great pastors in Ohio, the Reverend Billy Ball and the Reverend David Grubbs, committed to go with me. Since Peru's national language is Spanish, we enlisted Dr. Enrique Cepeda to come as well. We wanted to provide basic biblical training to these pastors, and provide them books and materials that would continue to help them long after we were gone.

That first conference in Lima proved to be a tremendous way to assist our national leaders. We put together a program to teach them how to prepare a sermon, how to study the Word, and how to develop a church. These pastors had never experienced anything like this before. We were feeding their souls, and they sat on the edge of those hard wooden benches for hours at a time soaking it up.

Knowing we had to provide resources for them, we enlisted some American Christians to provide funds to underwrite the gift of a concordance, a Bible dictionary, and one Eerdman's commentary. The pastors were thrilled. We were fulfilled. They received their certificate of completion the final night, and many were filled with emotion as to the gifts their ministry received. We knew in our hearts that this was something we had to repeat again and again. This was empowering the native pastors to reach their people for Christ.

It was during the next year's session in Peru when a little native pastor out of the jungles of the upper Amazon came to me. Pointing at the printed program, he showed me where it announced an upcoming session on the leadership of the Holy Spirit. "I know there is a Holy Spirit but I don't know anything about him," he said. That reconfirmed in my heart that what we were offering to these native pastors would surely have eternal results. They would go back into their villages, jungles, and remote areas better equipped, challenged anew, and filled with the inspiration to continue sharing the Gospel of Jesus Christ with those waiting to hear.

They held the answer for their people. That little pastor later told me of a schoolteacher in his area. They crossed paths one day on a trail to another village. Stopping to talk with this teacher, who was thrashing wheat at that time, the pastor asked the teacher if he knew Jesus. The teacher scratched his head and looked around, then replied, "I don't think he lives any where around here. I've never heard of him."

Our pastors' conferences grew quickly. Soon we were doing them in Colombia, Argentina, Panama, Haiti, Costa Rica, Nicaragua, Dominican Republic, and eventually on to Egypt, India, the Philippines, and China. What started as a dream became a very important part of serving national leaders. We have conducted an average of two conferences a year since 1983 and have taken over seventy American pastors to teach, serve, and get a burden for missions. More than 7,361 native pastors have been served.

As the conferences in India continued to escalate, Samuel Stephens began challenging his pastors to have a vision of their own. In November of 1992 he launched his VISION 2000 program. Looking at the pastors attending the conference, he caught a vision of what this group could do together by the year 2000 if they were challenged. Working

together they could plant 1,000 churches by the year 2000.

A year later Samuel admitted that his goal wasn't big enough. The goal was raised to 2,000 by the year 2000. In 1995 it was moved up to 5,000 churches by the year 2000. In 1997 Samuel realized their goal still wasn't big enough as they already planted 5,000 churches, so he challenged them to have 12,500 new churches by November 2000.

Many souls have been added to the Kingdom of God through the work and ministries of national pastors and leaders.

What a joy to serve men of God like these. What a privilege to be a part of their team. I've decided being a servant is really a wonderful and rewarding job.

A Church with a Servant Heart

There is a church in Wichita that showed its spirit of servanthood at the time of the Guatemala earthquake in 1976. February 4 of that year a major quake devastated that country from one side to the other. Not only were cities destroyed, but all forms of communication were impossible.

We worked extensively in Guatemala since 1972, taking teams to build churches in Tecpan, Quezaltenango, Dolores on Lake Amatitlan, San Luis, and other locations. With our medical boat, Sea Angel, on Lake Isabal, we built a medical clinic. We traveled to Coban in the north and built a hangar for Missionary Aviation Fellowship.

Because of our many friends now in Guatemala and the numerous times we were there building churches and schools, Chuck felt compelled to go immediately to see how he could help. He was able to enlist planes from Beech Aviation in Guatemala City because of our affiliation with Beech Aircraft in Wichita. He arranged to fly supplies into remote areas using roads for landing strips. Then he sent me some slides of the tremendous disaster the earthquake had caused.

Eastminster Presbyterian Church was having its annual missions festival during the time that Chuck was in Guatemala, so I called Dr. Paul Baumann, the chairman of the committee, to see if I could come to their missions dinner that night and show some pictures of Guatemala. He agreed.

Arriving a little ahead of time, I was introduced to the pastor. Pastor Kik wasn't too impressed, but he said that I could show the slides if I made it quick. A full evening had been planned and he didn't want to extend the time.

When my time came, I did as I was told and hurried through the pictures. As Pastor Kik saw these scenes of devastation, he began to wish I would slow down. I didn't know that, so I rushed on.

The next Tuesday was a special meeting of the church's board to finalize plans for their $500,000 addition to their sanctuary. As the board members were discussing the cost, one questioned, "How can we do this? We have brothers and sisters in Guatemala that have lost everything. How can we build this expensive addition to our building when they don't have any building at all? In other words, how can we have a 'Cadillac' when they don't even have a 'Volkswagen'?"

The board members decided to put their plans on hold and sent Pastor Kik and two session members, Bob Howard and Bob Schaffer, to Guatemala to assess the damage. Chuck met them in Guatemala where they discovered that every Presbyterian church there was damaged or destroyed.

With that report relayed back to the Eastminster board, and upon discovering there were no plans by their denomination for reconstruction, the board decided to reduce their building project from a $500,000 expansion to $150,000 and to raise $180,000 to replace every Presbyterian church in Guatemala. A special Sunday night congregational meeting was called where they presented this decision as Project Light, with the church voting overwhelmingly in favor of helping in Guatemala.

Our airplane was busy taking teams, from not only Wichita but across the United States, for the reconstruction of churches everywhere in Guatemala. Denominational lines didn't matter. What mattered was that there were brothers and sisters who were hurting and needed help. What mattered was that those people were without churches and we could help them have them again. We were sharing the light in the darkness. (We were picking up the towel of servanthood.)

There were many more opportunities that came our way when the Guatemala earthquake hit. Eastminster Presbyterian is just a good example of the types of churches we were working with. By that time we had a constituency across the United States with whom we partnered for help. From Florida to California, we loaded up our plane every three weeks taking a new team to Guatemala to rebuild churches and schools and do whatever was needed. We discovered that Christians want to be used of God, and knowing Christ, they enjoy developing a servant heart.

CHAPTER 5

COMPASSION: SEEING THE MULTITUDES
THROUGH THE EYES OF CHRIST

L ots of people were on the street that day in Bombay, India, but Chuck and I weren't worried; we knew that was normal for India. After all, India's *1 billion-plus* citizens live on a continent that contains more than one-sixth of Earth's population crowded into just 2 percent of its land mass.

Suddenly a whistle sounded. It must have been quitting time because people were pouring out of every door, completely filling the street, sidewalks, and the intersection, literally as far as the eye could see.

We climbed up on an elevated pier to get a better view of the whole scene. It was captivating: people swarmed everywhere. These were Indians with their brightly colored saris and churidars, their diverse ways and colorful culture. This was our first trip to India, so we looked in amazement. *Who are these people? Where are they coming from, and where are they going? What are their daily lives like? Did they know about Jesus Christ?*

I wondered what Jesus would have thought if he was standing in that place with us. The Scripture came to mind, "When he saw the crowds, he had compassion on them, because they were harassed and helpless, like sheep without a shepherd" (Matt 9:36, NIV). The Good Shepherd felt compassion for the multitudes he saw because they were lost. Here was another multitude in a country where fewer than 2 percent of the population is Christian. The vast majority were also "lost." In the United States, people often wear bracelets and other clothing items that carry the inscription, "W.W.J.D." What would Jesus do? No such images appeared in this crowd.

We became accustomed to being surrounded by multitudes. Back in the early 1980s when we first started leading mission trips to Beijing, China, I could create a multitude by just showing up. Everywhere I went in China, people stopped to stare at me, a strange-looking foreigner. My eyes were different. My skin was white. My clothes were strange, my hair brown and curly. Most Chinese hadn't seen many Westerners in person.

From 1964 to 1980 Chuck and I spent nearly all our time and ministry efforts in the Western Hemisphere. We took more than 4,000 people to Central America, the Caribbean, and South America on EyeWitness crusades or as work teams and even to help in disaster relief. There was still plenty to do there. But something had prompted me to take a small group to China, just as that country was opening up and visitors were finally being allowed.

In the China of 1981, tourists were very tightly controlled by the government. I brought seven people with me from the United States to Beijing. Since my group spoke English and since eight additional English-speaking tourists also arrived that day, the Chinese government put our groups together but left me as the leader. So now I had the eight of us, plus two from Australia, one from Denmark, one from New Zealand, a missionary couple from Japan, and two from Toledo, Ohio.

Everything was so different in Asia; it made the Rio Grande look like home. Our hotel was more like a youth camp, and all our activities were tightly planned and controlled. We were assigned a guide named Wang, a bus, and a bus driver. Wang would show us the Forbidden City, the Great Wall, Tiananmen Square, the Palace of Heaven, the Summer Palace, the Ming Tombs, and the Beijing Zoo.

During the week Wang asked me what kind of group we were.

"A Christian group," I replied.

"Is that a religion?" he responded. I was astounded. Here was a young man about twenty-eight-years-old who spoke excellent English, yet he knew little about the rest of the world, with no knowledge at all of Christianity. I was floored. I asked him if we could go to church on Sunday. The religious freedom we in the West take for granted wasn't present at that time, and indeed is still lacking in its fullness today, so I had wondered if the China Tourist Bureau would even allow us to go. Wang didn't know the answer, but said he would go back to the Bureau's office and find out.

The next morning Wang said we could go to church on Saturday night but not on Sunday because we were scheduled to go to the zoo on Sunday morning to see the Panda bears. He said, "There are two churches in Beijing (a city of 9 million people at that time). One is a Protestant church and one is a Catholic church. Which one would you like to go to?" We opted for the Protestant one, and on Saturday night he and the driver worked overtime to take us.

The church building, which was about thirty-by-sixty-feet, was filled to capacity. Since Wang came in with us, I thought this was a great opportunity for him to find out what Christianity is all about. Our group stayed together at the back so we wouldn't be in the way. Quietly I asked Wang, "Why aren't there any children here? Do they have them in another room?" I had visions of our American Sunday school classes in a separate building.

"It is illegal for anyone to go to church under the age of eighteen," Wang whispered. Again, the freedom to worship we have was highlighted in my heart.

As the service proceeded, I realized again that even if you don't know the language, you can enjoy the singing, know when they are reading scripture, and know when the sermon begins and ends. And you can worship in your heart along with the others. When the service concluded we shook hands with the pastor and climbed back on our bus.

I was anxious to get Wang's response to the service. Sitting in the front seat, I turned to him and asked, "Wang, what did you think of the service? Did you hear them talk about Jesus? Did you get an understanding of what Christianity is all about?"

I thought that since the service was conducted in his language, he would be full of questions and new insights.

"It didn't make much sense," he mumbled. "I didn't understand it."

I was so disappointed. Now what was I to do?

The Life-changing Question

It was then that Wang asked me that life-changing question. On the surface, it seemed so ordinary, yet later I would realize its eternal impact.

Wang simply asked, "Tell me, does your religion help you with your problems?"

What a question. Everyone in the world asks a question like this sometime in his or her life. Everyone has problems, and everyone needs a God who can solve problems. That's what we are all searching for, in one way or another. Now I had the challenge of answering Wang's question there in the darkness of the bus. I only had a twenty-minute ride to tell him all about God.

Since Wang had absolutely no knowledge of God, I started at the beginning. God the Creator. God making the Earth. God making mankind. God giving mankind a choice. Mankind sinning. God wanting to communicate with mankind. Then God sending messengers—the prophets—to bring mankind back to him. Sending more messengers until, out of God's love and compassion, he chose to send his only Son. In Chinese culture a son is the most prized possession a family can have.

"Wang, God loves this world so much that he sent his only Son, so that anyone who will believe in him will have eternal life," I told him. "Wang, would you like to have eternal life?"

Now who is going to say no to that question? And Wang didn't either. He began asking all sorts of questions about eternal life.

The bus arrived back at our hotel. As our group filed off the bus, I offered, "Wang, I have a little book up in my room that tells about eternal life. It is called John. Would you like to have it?"

"Yes, thank you," he responded without hesitation.

How I thanked the Lord that he had prepared me for this opportunity. A friend in Hong Kong gave me a supply of Bibles and copies of the Gospel of John to deliver to a brother in Shanghai before our trip began.

Wang was pleased to have the book. When he came the next morning to take us to the zoo and then to the airport for our flight to Shanghai, he told me he already read about half of it and was eager to read the rest. We were only able to continue our discussion briefly before we arrived at the airport. As we turned to say good-bye one last time, my lips and my heart were saying, "Wang, read the rest of the book. It will tell you Who loves you and Who can help you with your problems."

As the plane climbed into the bright blue Beijing sky, my thoughts drifted back to that morning's excursion. We had gone to Tiananmen Square after visiting the zoo; the Square was alive with people going every which way. At that time all Chinese, men and women alike, wore blue Mao jackets and blue Mao pants. In a crowd they formed a sea of blue. The light faces and different clothing colors of our group stood out. In just a few minutes we had drawn a crowd of staring faces. That Sunday morning about seventy-five Chinese people surrounded me. Their stares went right through me. Here was another multitude, who like Wang, had little or no knowledge of Christ. The Lord was talking to my heart.

Suddenly, it was as if these people were all asking me Wang's question, "Tell me, does your religion help you with your problems? If so, why don't you tell us? If you don't tell us, who will? How will we ever know?"

Compassion for the multitudes—that's what Jesus felt. Now I felt it. My heart was broken. I could only speak English. Even if I did know how to speak Chinese, I wouldn't be allowed to proclaim Christ there. Not in Tiananmen Square in 1981, not without going to jail. What was I supposed to do?

The Lord turned my dilemma that day into a special burden. I was indelibly changed amid that sea of China blue. He gave me his love and concern for the Chinese.

Through the Eyes of Christ

Since that day whenever I take a group of believers out of the United States, I ask them to look at the people through the eyes of Christ. I challenge them not to look as a tourist would, or at their commodities as a comparison shopper, but rather to look into the eyes of the people as Jesus did. My primary goal for short-term mission trips, as well as of our lifelong growth as Christians, became what World Vision founder Bob Pierce so beautifully expressed, that our hearts be broken by the things that break the heart of God.

In 1987 I went to Salem, India, to meet with my friend Samuel Stephens, who operated the India Gospel League. One morning he put me in his car and said, "Donna, I want you to see some lepers today." I had no idea there were lepers in India. We read about lepers in the Bible but most of us think that disease is eradicated today, right? Wrong.

Samuel continued, "We are going to the Anderson School campus where there will be many lepers waiting for us. Today is our monthly feeding program. Each month we invite the lepers in, give them a good meal of rice and meat and vegetables, and then give them either a blanket or some other form of covering, along with a bit of money. These people you will meet live in the streets. When someone contracts leprosy, he is sent from his home to the streets. We are planning to build a place for some lepers as soon as we get the money for it. Then they can have a roof over their heads and a place besides the gutter to lie down."

When we arrived they were seated on the ground in orderly rows. I had expected twenty-five or so, but no—there were perhaps 300. The natural tourist instinct compelled me to get a picture. As we moved through the rows, I saw lepers who were young and old, male and female. Some lacked toes, others had a foot or leg missing. Many had no fingers at all. Some were without a nose, others with an ear gone. Gross deformities were common. And there were children—babies, toddlers, young children. I put the camera away.

These precious people had become the untouchables in society. Carriers of a contagious disease, they were universally shunned. Their life consisted of walking the streets with nowhere to live, no job, no income, no food. Beggars. Living off others' garbage, combing through trash for food. If their illness had been detected and treated at its onset, it could have been cured. At this stage, there was no hope, no future.

Samuel and his team placed a large banana leaf in front of each leper. Banana leaves in India are used like we use paper plates. They began ladling some curry, rice and meat onto each person's leaf.

This scene impacted the inner recesses of my heart. I had to either help or leave. There was no way I could just observe. I chose to carry the pots and ladle the curry. My questions and thoughts spun quickly from my heart. *Why was I born in the United States of sound mind and body? Why was I blessed with loving Christian parents and a lifestyle that included medical care and treatment? And who told me, my parents, and my grandparents about the Savior?*

My eyes focused on one young mother sitting with her baby among the others. *How did she get here? How did she contract leprosy? What does it feel like to be an outcast?* She had lost all the fingers on her right hand and her fingers were shorter than normal on her left. *How can she take care of that beautiful baby girl? Will the baby contract leprosy too?* My mind was overloaded; I couldn't conceive of life like that. The mother looked at me and smiled in simple gratitude that I was serving her food.

Dipping the curry, moving on down first one row and then another, I felt my eyes grow wet with tears. My heart was crying out to the Lord: *What can I do to help? And how can I not only help these with leprosy, but also help those oppressed with their sins with no knowledge of the Savior? Lord, I too see the multitudes, and you have given me compassion for them.*

When we have eyes that see the multitudes, the Lord can lead us into new ventures and adventures. We are open to things we probably would never have thought of before. We can sense the Lord's guidance for our lives: to move on, to take a new direction, to be a part of the solution, to make changes, to dream dreams, to have visions, to plan, to produce, to have compassion, to make a difference.

Seeing the Need

The Reverend Samuel Stephens' schools for children are intriguing. Drawing their heritage from British rule, they have a lot of formality and stateliness. Visitors are met by selected children who offer a lei of roses as welcome. They give beautifully memorized words of greeting. When our teams come, an honor guard leads us across their school campus to a reviewing stand with all the students seated on the ground in straight rows. A beautiful formal program follows as they perform plays, dances, songs, gymnastics, and recitations. Jesus would have loved that experience of watching this multitude of children.

The Reverend Stephens and his ministry colleagues labor in a mission field where Christianity stands out starkly. They work in predominantly Hindu villages. The lifestyle of the people is the same in many ways as in the days when Jesus walked this earth. They live from day to day, from hand to mouth. Most have no modern telecommunications or knowledge of the outside world. They are caught in the oppressive caste system (a strict social structure that controls economic and social progress). They worship Hindu idols and gods whom they believe control all aspects of their lives, mainly through fear and superstition. Some offer their sons or daughters to the Hindu gods, perhaps by walking on coals of fire or puncturing their jaws with metal rods six feet long or even by becoming temple prostitutes.

Then they hear the news of a Savior. Samuel Stephens and his teams of "barefoot pastors" begin by using the Jesus film, which is based on the Gospel of Luke and produced by Campus Crusade for

Christ. Their reaction is much the same as we read in the Gospels. Many come eagerly to the Savior, but others turn away.

As villagers respond, a fellowship group forms to start Bible study and literacy classes. As the group grows and The Reverend Samuel Stephens finds funds from his partners here in the United States, a church building is constructed. This becomes the "Life Center" in the village where, as the ministry develops, villagers are also instructed in primary health care, maternal health care, and vocations.

The dedication of each twenty-five-by-fifty-foot church building is of major importance, a time of celebration done with much pomp and ceremony. Most of the local villagers show up for this event; they are the multitude. Those officiating lead everyone around the church singing, have a dedication prayer, and cut the ribbon across the entryway. The villagers then enter a festive and decorated concrete block building. The Good News is proclaimed. These villagers' lives are forever changed; Christ—through God's people who had eyes to see the multitudes as he did—came by and had compassion on them.

The Multitudes Around Us

There have been other multitudes in my life; sometimes I've looked for them and other times they've jumped out at me. It isn't the *size* of the multitudes that is important, it's what is in their eyes. Their needs.

I remembered the encounter Chuck and I had with two Taiwanese nuclear engineering graduate students who just arrived in the United States to study at the University of Cincinnati. A reception for foreign students was being held, and we drove the forty miles to see if we could make some friends.

We met Jack and Daniel (their American names) in the reception line. These two young men had only been in Cincinnati one week. They needed help, and we decided to begin helping them that same evening. We took them to the supermarket to help them understand our Western concepts of buying and selling food. Wow, that was an experience! They never saw a store like that before and were so intrigued with the many cans, boxes, bottles, products, packages, and all. That was an education in itself for them.

The next Saturday we brought them to our house for dinner. They were happy to have American friends. We showed them around and answered their numerous questions about our style of living. Then, sitting down to dinner, Chuck explained to them that we always stop and thank the Lord for our food before we eat. This was new to them and raised lots of questions about the Lord, which we were very happy to answer. That was a most interesting and enjoyable experience as we shared Christ with them and chatted about our respective cultures. I was amazed to hear them asking us essentially the same question that Wang had asked me back in Beijing three years prior: "Does your religion help you with your problems?"

We invited these two young men several times for meals, and questions about God always surfaced. On one occasion, shortly before Christmas, we had our Christmas tree up. They asked questions about our celebration. Then came the question, "Is Santa Claus the father of Jesus?" How confusing our culture is to those who don't have a Christian background. At Easter we also had to explain how the Easter Bunny came into the picture, trying to explain the mixture of Christian and secular elements in our culture. By discussing these questions, Chuck and I came to understand yet another ministry of being there for foreign students to help them find their way to the Lord.

There are multitudes all around us, not just the huge pressing crowds in Bombay or China. Consider the groups at McDonald's, or the Korean family that owns the shoe repair shop, or that new Ethiopian family that just moved in down the block. We need to open our eyes to all the Lord wants to show us about ministry, both here and abroad. It's like the time Jesus met two blind men on the Jericho road: Jesus stopped and called them. "What do you want me to do for you?" he asked. "Lord," they answered, "we want our sight." Jesus had compassion on them and touched their eyes. Immediately they received their sight and followed him (Matt 20:32–34, NIV).

CHAPTER 6
TRUST: FINDING GOD'S PLANS

A Mountain Within

Sometimes the mountain is not outside ourselves, but within. In 1983 Chuck was complaining of extreme fatigue and lack of energy. He also seemed to have a pain in his chest at times, which he called a "spell." He finally went to our local doctor who, after tests and an examination, said Chuck had a heart problem. We had a friend in Wichita who was a heart specialist, so we flew there to get his opinion. It wasn't any better and he suggested we go to the famed Mayo Clinic in Rochester, Minnesota. At Mayo they told Chuck he had cardiomyopathy (where the heart muscles deteriorate and enlarge; they can't pump effectively and it's just a matter of time before you die). They said there was nothing they could do. That was hard to take.

It wasn't long after that that Chuck's condition worsened and he felt he needed to resign as president of Project Partner. We had founded Project Partner in 1968 and he had been the president for fifteen years. This was quite a blow for both of us. When he resigned, I did too, as we had always done things together. The board of directors took three months in prayer and searching and then asked me to be president. That was not a question I ever considered. After prayer and discussion with Chuck, I consented to take that role.

I already started the ministry of training native pastors and seeing the remarkable results these conferences brought and continued to develop this ministry in many countries in the Western Hemisphere. In March 1987, I went to Haiti to hold another pastor's conference. Chuck seemed to be getting worse.

He actually looked gray and was so tired and weak. Oh, how I hated to leave him behind for those ten days.

On my return, however, I felt something was different. As I stepped down from the plane I saw my husband waiting for me, as usual. But there was something different. There was a glow, a certain something that was missing ever since he'd been struck down with this heart problem. I was excited but powerfully curious.

"What happened to you?" I asked.

"Just wait. Wait 'til we get to the car."

I tried to wait, but he was off at a pace that startled me. Chuck's long legs had always propelled him so fast I usually had to run to keep up. But the heart condition had slowed him to my speed these past four years. Walking was a labor; stairs were steep mountains to him. Now here I was, trotting again.

"Hey, slow down!" I yelled playfully above the airport rumble.

In the car Chuck smiled but was silent. I relived the months of tests, the trips to the Mayo Clinic, and the steady decline in his health. I remembered the heartbreak as I saw him waste away before my eyes.

Quietly, thoughtfully, he said, "Donna, I think I've been healed." What a pleasant, heart-lifting bombshell. Chuck was serious. With tears in his eyes he tried to answer my avalanche of questions. *When? How? Where?*

It happened on the day after I'd left for Haiti. In our back yard he'd had another of his spells ... weakness, pain, and shortness of breath. He made it inside to our couch. "When I awoke some time later," Chuck told me, "I remembered I was invited to dinner and thought I'd better call and cancel.

"Gingerly I got up and planned to creep across the room to the phone. But then, to my amazement, I realized I felt no pain. I straightened up, stretched, and walked around the room. I was astounded; it felt like a dream. My plan to call and cancel the dinner began to fade. *Maybe I'll shower and see how that feels, I thought to myself.*"

My husband showered, shaved, and dressed. No pain. He went to dinner. He felt fine. Being cautious, he decided not to say anything to anyone about his recovery, for fear it would be a false alarm.

The next day was Sunday. Chuck's attacks always left him weak for days. Now he felt like heading out to church on the day after his latest attack. He felt so great that he went back for the evening service.

While I was still in Haiti, Chuck got back to work. It was catch-up time. We lived on a large lot with plenty of trees and brush near Springboro, Ohio. There was always tons of maintenance to be done. He replaced windows in the barn, made major repairs in another building, and caught up on four years worth of odd jobs that sickness forced him to postpone.

After he told me his story there in the car, we hugged and cried. We held each other tightly. Bountiful thanks to God filled our hearts. And then we became strangely quiet.

We were both thinking of all the people who prayed. We recalled the tearful times at the altar with dozens of friends around us. We thought of the notes, the phone calls, the people who had "just stopped by" to pray with him. Out of a clear blue sky he'd received this special miracle.

Was it real? Was it a healing or just a quirk of fate or random circumstance? Could it be permanent? So we waited, worked, prayed, and just trusted God with it. Two weeks later Chuck was asked to share with the church what had happened. Boldly, Chuck gave the report and thanked God for the healing he extended to him.

We began to wonder about Chuck's medication. Should he take it? Shouldn't his cardiologist be consulted? What role did medicine have in this, and what role faith? We truly wrestled with these points and decided he should visit the cardiologist again.

Going to the cardiologist was a shock. He didn't believe Chuck's story. "Just come back to see me when you're in pain again," he said with what seemed to be a bit of cynicism. So, on our own, we just started reducing his pain pills. A little reduction at a time; then more. Then one day Chuck forgot to take his medicine. And that was the end of that. No pills, no pain. Day followed day. Feeling good, working hard, taking no medicine. Fifty days, then one hundred. Two hundred, and then a whole year.

Chuck had spent years as a pilot, but when the heart condition was diagnosed his license had been suspended. At the end of a year after his healing, he decided he wanted to recertify to fly again.

Chuck was examined, tested, and quizzed. The FAA doctors and examiners turned him every way but loose and finally gave him a clean bill of health. He took the required tests yet, in the typical process of governmental red tape, after eight months he still didn't have his license. At last it came in the mail. Clutching the paper in his hand, Chuck yelled with a big grin, "I can fly again!" It was a joyful yell of praise to God.

The Next Step

"Now what do I do with my life?" Chuck asked over his morning cup of tea. Because of his heart trouble, Chuck's life was radically changed. He was living day to day, living only to endure, to survive. Work, church responsibilities, and family chores were shelved. Now, with a renewed sense of life, he wondered what was ahead.

"What do I really want to do?" he asked me with a smile. Each new breath was a gift from Heaven. This man I loved was facing a new kind of life.

Almost as if God had actually sent a telegram, the answer came. I planned a trip to China and he decided to go. There he saw the urgent medical poverty, the absence of basic materials and equipment, and the lack of what we in the West consider basic medical skills. We asked the local believers what they needed.

"We need help. We need a medical team to show us how to improve," came the plea from our Chinese leader.

The light dawned for Project Partner. "We can take medical people to places where they are needed," Chuck concluded. And so a brand new phase of his life was born.

Back home he quickly put together a team of Christian medical personnel from the Cincinnati area. Off this team went to China, then another team to Peru, and another to Nicaragua. For five wonderful years Chuck continued to walk by faith in this new direction the Lord gave him.

God's Divine Appointment

The Lord gave me a great burden for the Chinese people when I was there in Tiananmen Square on my first trip to China. It was then when those questions came, "Does your religion help you with your problems? If you have a religion that helps, why don't you tell us? If you don't tell us, who will?"

In 1984, some three years after my first trip to China the Lord challenged me. I was in the Philippines at this time, leading a conference for national pastors. Chuck and I had brought two pastors from the United States—Jim Burchett from Cincinnati and Randy Rohr from Michigan—to train Filipino pastors. After they experienced the ministry opportunities in the Pacific, we headed to Hong Kong where I wanted them to gain a better understanding of the various cultures in Asia.

Our contacts in Hong Kong were Arthur and Betty Gee. I met them on our first trip three years earlier as they were the regional directors of Partners International and offered to help me. This time they said that they had a special man they wanted me to meet. He lived in Macau, where he pastored a church. I learned to welcome new opportunities, and Macau was a place I had not been.

Macau was a Portuguese province only one mile square. It was comprised mostly of Chinese who had fled the communists on the mainland. A narrow strip of land connects Macau and China, and according to an agreement between Portugal and China, it reverted to China in 1999.

Have you ever been on a jetfoil? That is the better way to travel from Hong Kong to Macau. Otherwise, the regular boat trip takes three to four hours. The jetfoil takes only one hour to arrive. Its hull rises above the water on special underwater wings and flies along much faster than traditional boats. It is much like riding on a low-flying airplane, skimming above the waves at a height of about six to ten feet.

Arthur and Betty's special friend, Pastor Loo, was waiting for us as we came through immigration. He was a tall man with a welcoming smile on his face. He didn't speak English and I didn't know how to speak Chinese, so our greetings to each other after the introduction were quite limited. He wanted us to follow him. He was an energetic man and walked rapidly ahead of us with great purpose in his stride.

We crowded into Pastor Loo's medium-size van and he started showing us the basics of Macau and the historical landmarks. The province was captured by the Portuguese back in the 1500s and their influence was everywhere. Among other places, he took us to the cemetery where John Morrison, the first missionary to China and the man who translated the Bible into Chinese, was buried.

Of course we went to Pastor Loo's church, located only two blocks from a McDonald's, right in the middle of Macau. The church was impressive because of its location and size, but it wasn't until we were in his office that I realized I was meeting a new challenge. God had brought me here to show me another mountain to climb by faith.

Pastor Loo showed me the plans and blueprints for a church building in mainland China. "How can that be?" I asked. "The Chinese government won't allow churches to be built, will they? I thought they didn't allow any religion."

Pastor Loo had that all figured out. "This church building," he said, "would be on the edge of a cemetery. It would be classified as a funeral chapel initially, but it would also be used as a church building for the area."

Now came his request for help. "Will you help us build this building for the Chinese people?"

Well, I certainly wanted to, but there was absolutely no money at Project Partner for anything in China. The money at Project Partner was designated for other places. *How could I possibly do anything here?* Not wanting to offend him with a negative reply, I asked, "How much will it cost and about how long will it take?"

His reply was very matter-of-fact. "This project will take a little less than a year and cost around $12,000." I knew I didn't have a dime to help him. I also knew that if he said he needed $12,000, it would take additional money to raise the $12,000. *How should I reply?*

I took the right way out but, actually, it was more of an excuse for me than the right answer. I told him I would pray about it.

We spent the rest of the day seeing more of Macau and some of the other churches he pastored, but I couldn't concentrate. I was too busy thinking of that mainland Chinese church. His plan was unheard-of; it was bold. There were no new churches in China and there hadn't been any since the Cultural Revolution.

My thoughts went round and round in my head, like a conversation between two opposing parties:

Can I help him?

No, there's no way.

But what if I tried?

Are you out of your mind?

Maybe I could get some new churches and Christians at home to help.

This is a bigger project than you can handle.

But this project is so worthy; it looks like it would really produce fruit for the Lord.

It would be pretty bad to start this and not be able to finish it. You'd really have egg on your face.

But it really needs to be done and if I don't help, who will? It might never happen if I don't help now.

You really think that you can find this kind of money?

Pastor Loo took us back to the jetfoil for the return to Hong Kong. This was it; I would soon be leaving this precious man of God, possibly never to see him again until Heaven. What was I to do? I felt an urgency.

As we left his car, I turned to him and stammered, "Pastor Loo, if you will give me a year, I will raise that money for you and help you build that church."

Well, I had made a decision. I hoped it was right.

Pastor Loo smiled and thanked me for my offer to try to help. He had an expression that almost said that he was expecting my offer all along. God was in it, I think he knew that.

It really wasn't as hard as I thought it would be. China was beginning to open up. People were very interested in what was happening there. It was easy to get the ear of churches and Christians, and the Lord provided the money through his people. Money came from Tulsa, Daytona Beach, Cincinnati, Wichita, Dayton, Danville, San Bernardino, Marion, St. Louis, Liberal, Fort Wayne, and other cities. As those contributions arrived in our mailbox, they were sent to China.

Pastor Loo was good at helping me. He responded quickly each time by sending me pictures of the construction. It was really happening. A church in mainland China in 1984 was actually being built, and by faith and trust I had a part in it.

CHAPTER 7

GUIDANCE: WHEN YOU CAN'T SEE
THE NEXT STEP

Who would have thought that I would be in Nanning, China, with eight Chinese government officials? This was 1994, thirteen years after that first trip to China and ten years after Pastor Loo challenged me to help build that first church building. Project Partner's ministry expanded to include medical teams and donations of medical equipment. American doctors, nurses, and dentists were giving their time to travel to foreign countries to offer free medical clinics and train local medical personnel. Chuck took our first medical team to Xingling in 1989 along with a container load of medical equipment. Since then he took another medical team to do some training with Chinese doctors in Zhanjiang. We also sent two more containers of medical equipment for their hospitals. This trip was the result of a request of the Chinese government for a medical team in Hechi. Our motivation was to help Pastor Loo and I never expected this kind of attention by the Chinese government.

Ten of us were seated in a special room at a lovely old hotel. The head of government affairs, Mr. Xin was providing this special luncheon for me, and my interpreter, Caleb Loo. This was a great honor. Mr. Xin was seated to my left and around the table were seven members of his staff. Caleb was on my right, ready to translate for me. Chinese functions typically include many toasts. Mr. Xin started by asking me if I drank rice wine. "No, I don't," was my cautious reply.

Knowing that I was a Christian he asked, "Do Christians in America drink wine?"

"Some do and others don't." I cautiously responded.

"We can use guava juice. Would that be all right?" he graciously asked.

"I think the guava juice would be very good," I replied.

The first toast was for me, the second for him, and we went on and on with one toast after another. Then came soup, the first course of a long meal. The beautiful tiny Chinese bowls held delicious steaming broth with some unfamiliar pieces of meat. It tasted pretty good to me.

"Did you like the soup?" Mr. Xin asked.

"Yes, it was very good," I replied.

"I had hoped that you would like it. Did you know that it was cobra soup?" he responded.

I was glad he told me after I ate rather than before. From years of traveling in foreign countries, I have developed a philosophy about food. First, I never ask what I am eating, because sometimes it is better not to know. Second, I never look in the kitchen because it might take my appetite away quickly. Third, I remind myself that I am there with the Lord. And fourth, I pray for wisdom, lots of grace, and safety.

Using Opportunities

Mr. Xin asked me what I did back in America. When people ask me that, I often stop and consider what they could relate to the best before responding. In this case, the Lord planted in my heart to tell him the reason I began working in China in the first place. This was my opportunity. I knew that in his position he could not ask me about Christianity or even religion. But I could tell him my encounter with Wang and Tiananmen Square back in 1981 and how the Lord put China on my heart. I could present him with Wang's question, "Does your religion help you with your problems?" And then I could give him the enthusiastic answer: yes.

So out came the story of Wang and his question. I gave him a short version of the biblical truths about God, sin, God sending prophets or messengers, John 3:16, and eternal life.

Wang obviously never heard John 3:16 before and the fact that God loved him and wanted him to believe in Jesus. He listened politely to my story, but of course could not make a response. A Chinese government official could not at that time choose to be a Christian. But the seed had been planted, he was most cordial, and we had a delightful time together.

Back then I didn't know about the Chinese system of *guangi*. It seems that in their culture, you don't have any response or relationship to anyone until some kind of bridge is built between you. There is no recognition of another person in any situation unless a bridge is there first. This bridge is built either by an intermediary or by you doing something very special. My bridge was bringing a team of medical doctors to teach in their hospital in Hechi. We also sent in a ship container of medical equipment. Sending those two gifts, the team and the equipment, put me into a special relationship. I gained the respect of the government leaders. This was the reason for this special luncheon.

I'll probably never again meet Mr. Xin or his team of government officials. But that opportunity came to me, and the Lord guided my response. Guidance from the Lord is so very special. He doesn't give it to us in five-year plans. It is usually one step at a time. The Lord uses people or circumstances to plant his plans in your mind and then your task is to respond. Now I pray there will be another who will come into his life to lead him to know Christ as his savior. As Paul wrote in 1 Corinthians 3:6, "I planted the seed, Apollos watered it, but God made it grow."

Turning Corners

The question I have learned to keep asking is, What does the Lord want us to do next? I have discovered that the Lord is never finished with us. He always has more. I am sure he will always have more until he takes us home to him. God continues to put opportunities in our path and his plans in our hearts.

When Project Partner with Christ was first formed, our primary purpose was to take people to see and experience God at work in other cultures. We named these trips EyeWitness Crusades. Since 1964 we have sponsored hundreds of them. Those first bus trips were EyeWitness Crusades before we knew what to call them. Whenever we could, we loaded up that bus with people from across the United States to go with us to Mexico to see what the Lord was doing in that country.

In 1968 that divine discontent set in, and we felt we should go for an airplane so we could go to more places than just Mexico. That plane provided EyeWitness Crusades across all of Central America and the Caribbean. It helped us turn a corner on the next phase of our ministry. Those Christian leaders needed help. They wanted to build a church or a school or a clinic or something else and didn't have the resources. Through those trips we came to see what was going on in a country, meet pastors, and have worship and prayer with them.

It was 1971, ten years after the Lord had taken us on our Rio Grande experience of entering a different culture. It was seven years after we had bought the bus and started helping our people see that the Lord was alive and active with other cultures. We were about to turn a corner again, getting more involved with missions and people and their world.

I remember the day one of those pastors told us that his congregation was really growing but they didn't have any place to worship. They bought some land and were trying to save some funds to build a simple place of worship. Standing there in the bright sun that morning in the village of Dolores in Guatemala, we knew the Lord was guiding us in a new direction. There were those colorfully dressed Indian women, descendants of the ancient Mayans, going on their way to market with loaded baskets on their heads. Often a child was hanging onto their hand-woven skirts or wrapped in a blanket on their backs. The men in their distinctive Indian garb passed by also, most with a machete in hand. We had nothing in common with these people culturally, but we had a lot in common with them through the love of God. We were beginning to understand their need.

As the pastor was talking about their need for a church building, Chuck looked over at me and said, "We can do that. We can help them have a church building. All we have to do is to ask people to come with us, bringing their work clothes and tools, and we can help them build that church." With that our workcamp program was started.

We had a small mailing list, but it was a start. We scheduled the first work camp for Dolores, Guatemala, set the dates, figured out a price that would cover all expenses, and set out to find people who would be willing to take two weeks and go with us to build that church. Our biggest response came from Alliance, Ohio, so we flew the plane there to pick up the team and then down to New Orleans. From there our path was to Merida, Mexico, and then direct to Guatemala City.

The team of workers brought sleeping bags with them and tools. Part of the crew was to locate the materials, another group was to lay the blocks, and a group of women were to do the cooking for the team. We built that first church out of cement block with a tin roof.

Our workcamp approach was simple. Every day started and ended with a prayer circle. The key to our productivity was building relationships with the native workers. We wanted to know them, to work side by side with them, to help them build their church. We soon discovered that we didn't need to finish a building. We only needed to get the walls and roof up and perhaps the doors on. They could finish it from there, so it really became their building and not the building of the North Americans.

During these times it was a joy and privilege to have worship services with the natives. They were so kind, so generous, and so gracious. They were always bringing us something as a gift—maybe a mango, or an ear of corn, or even a chicken for the pot that evening. Great relationships were formed, and when the teams from the States went home they began saving their money for the next workcamp.

Those early workcamps were thrilling. People were excited about going and getting their hands dirty for the Lord. With our airplane we could take as many as forty people. We learned our way around all of Central America, and the Lord showed us many needs. People across the United States were finding out about these workcamps and were wanting to be a part.

From 1971 to 1978 we flew that plane to Guatemala and built churches and schools. We built a hangar for Missionary Aviation Fellowship in Coban, and we went to El Salvador and built churches. We built a mission school in Siguatepeque, Honduras, as well as churches in Panama on both sides of the isthmus, in Costa Rica, and in Belize.

Finding a Way

In December of 1972 Nicaragua suffered a disastrous earthquake. It struck Managua, a city of a half million people, killing more than thirty thousand while completely devastating the heart of the city. In January, Chuck and I took a team to Guatemala City to work with Isai Calderon, a native leader. There, waiting for us at Isai's church, was a leading pastor from Nicaragua.

"I am Misael Lopez from Managua. I called Isai Calderon for help with the earthquake and he told me you were coming and perhaps you could help us."

Misael was exhausted physically and emotionally and consumed with anxiety and concern for his people. He was the leader of the Nicaraguan A.M.E.N. (*Associacion Misionero Evangelica Nacional*) churches. The earthquake destroyed sixteen of their churches, which affected more than two thousand of his people alone. With deep concern, Chuck listened as Misael told him of the night the earth shook, and about the destruction and horror left by its frenzy.

"That night," Misael began, "we were on the second floor of our home. My wife, Amina, and my daughter were asleep. I was having trouble going to sleep, and at 12:30 A.M. I got up to take a pill so I could get some rest. I put the pill into my hand, but I never got to swallow it. The earthquake threw me down. I thought we were all going to die.

"My wife and I ran outside. We were both knocked to the ground and couldn't get up. We saw the house and the store next door collapse. It was a huge warehouse filled with electrical appliances that were falling, metal scratching, rocks rolling down, wood cracking. The noise, it was terrible. And then there was the screaming and the crying.

"I ran to find my daughter. I found her trapped inside our home. I ran next door to get some help to release her, but my neighbor had a large beam across his chest. I ran to the next door, but that neighbor was dead. I ran across the street and found those neighbors unconscious. Later they died. I ran back to my house and I could smell gas, so I searched to find the valve and turn it off. Finally, somehow, I released my daughter from where she was trapped and ran back to help my neighbor, but he was dead. There were two dead people in our yard.

"I carried a woman with two broken legs almost five miles to the hospital, but when we got there the hospital was gone. I had to put the woman down on the ground ... to die." Misael was so overcome with emotion that he waited before he continued.

"That night thirty thousand people died. Downtown huge fires burned and we could not put them out. The city burned for days. People, including us, tried to get out of Managua, but could not. We stayed five days in the yard with no food or water. By this time thousands more were dead because of hunger, thirst, and injury.

"I finally got a call out to Pastor Isai to see if he could bring food to Managua. I told him we had no food, no water, nothing. I begged him to come, and he told me you were coming. Please, Reverend Thomas, will you come and *ponga sus ojos en Managua* (put your eyes on Managua)?"

Chuck and I left the next day to "put our eyes" on Managua. We saw devastation unlike anything we ever saw before. Awash with waves of helplessness, we surveyed the tragedy. This disaster was greater than we imagined, the need of this pastor greater than we could handle. And the earth was still trembling. We decided to start by going to the United States embassy to meet with Ambassador Turner Sheldon, and we told Misael of our plan.

"Reverend Thomas, this is impossible!" Misael responded sadly. "He will be too busy, everyone wants to see him. It is impossible."

Chuck was sure that this was the first step and was determined to go. Arriving at the embassy, we discovered the building was gone. It too was destroyed. We finally found the ambassador's temporary office, only to find it surrounded by soldiers who spoke Spanish exclusively. Just when Chuck depleted all the ways he knew to make himself understood, the ambassador's secretary, an American, happened by and intervened. Politely she listened as he told her his reasons for needing to meet with the ambassador.

She told us we could wait and take a chance on seeing him, so we sat down to wait it out. In about an hour a limousine pulled up to the curb. Chuck recognized the man getting out as the ambassador.

"Sir, I need to talk with you. I must talk with you."

"Come on in."

"Sir, I want to help here in Managua. We have a large airplane and we can bring in a lot of supplies and many things to help. I need to see General Somoza and get his permission to bring in the airplane minus all the red tape. Can you help me get in to see him?"

"Impossible."

"Well, can't we try?"

Tentatively shaking his head, the ambassador sighed deeply. "Well," he said, "I'm going to the Security Council meeting at 2:00 this afternoon. Of course, there will be hundreds of people there, but still, I am supposed to get the chance to speak with him," his voice trailed off.

Later that day the ambassador reported back to us. "I'm sorry. I didn't get to speak to General Somoza, but I did get to tell the vice president about you. He has invited you to the next Security Council meeting tomorrow afternoon."

Misael and Amina could not believe their ears when we told them. But the next day Misael and Amina went with Chuck and me to the military compound housing of General Somoza. It was a hot day and there were soldiers everywhere. They stopped our car to find out who we were.

"I am Chuck Thomas, Project Partner, USA, and I've been invited by the vice president to attend the Security Council meeting this afternoon." After radioing inside, the guard motioned for us to proceed. I was left in the car as Chuck, Misael, and Amina were led past ornate surroundings and highly polished and extremely military soldiers, on past a huge high fence, across well-kept grounds, to the outdoor meeting place. They were escorted to wooden bleachers to sit with another hundred spectators. Before them, sitting on folding chairs at a long table, were the dignitaries.

As General Somoza was announced, everyone stood at attention until he was seated. Dressed in khaki trousers and a short-sleeved white shirt with gold epaulettes bearing the stars of a general, he appeared to be very tired.

Watching the proceedings carefully, Amina interpreted for Chuck what was said and explained what was going on. Reports were given and accepted quickly. Spain was prepared to give a large amount of money to repair damaged schools. Mexico was sending money and a caravan of food. The United States was prepared to begin rebuilding the water system. Suddenly, it was all over. The president stood, turned quickly, and left.

Chuck was not willing to let it go. He walked quickly toward the palace with Amina and Misael scurrying to keep up with him. They were frightened as this was not the proper way to do things in Nicaragua. At the front steps the guard stopped them. "Who are you?" he demanded of Chuck.

"I am the Reverend Chuck Thomas of Project Partner, USA and I must see President Somoza."

"Do you have an appointment?"

"No sir, I do not, but I must see him," Chuck insisted.

"But you do not have an appointment?" the guard repeated.

"No. I do not. But please, is there someone else I can speak to? I really must speak with him," Chuck pleaded.

Shaking his head he barked, "Wait here."

Another military man was summoned, and still another. Finally one who spoke excellent English came. Chuck recognized him as one of the gentlemen who was seated at the table during the Security Council meeting. This one had a different expression on his face as he listened intently while Chuck again stated his request for a meeting with General Somoza. This one had authority, and he was interested in just what this insistent American wanted.

"Why do you wish such a meeting?"

"We have a large airplane. We can bring in food supplies, medical supplies, and building equipment, and we have people who are willing to come and work. There are more than two thousand people connected with the A.M.E.N. churches who we desperately wish to help. They, in turn, will help us aid other people in need here. I must see the president, as I know he is the only one who can give me permission to bring my airplane in without going through all the hassle at customs. This is what I need."

"You are right, you must see the president for this request," he agreed.

Quickly they followed the man as he abruptly turned and hurried up the steps to the portico, where he motioned for them to wait. Shortly, a uniformed soldier appeared before them. "The president will see you now," he said with a slight bow in Chuck's direction. "But you must leave your camera here."

Chuck followed him into a small room where he was carefully searched before being ushered into a lovely reception room. There he sat alone and waited until a woman came to show him into a small room where a guard stood at attention. She introduced Chuck to the guard and then left. The guard turned, opened another door, and motioned Chuck inside. To his amazement, as the door opened to let him enter, two other doors opened, one on either side of a large desk, and in each doorway stood a uniformed guard holding a Thompson submachine gun. Besides the desk, the only other furnishings in the room were two chairs. Chuck was instructed to remain standing before the desk until requested to sit, and to speak only when spoken to.

When the President entered, the guard presented Chuck to him. The two guards holding the machine guns stayed at attention.

"Be seated," General Somoza said. "I apologize for having to take your camera away from you. You'll get it back when you leave." The General spoke in flawless English.

"That's perfectly all right," Chuck said. "I guess my ego was getting the best of me anyway. I just hoped that I could get a picture of you."

"That can be arranged. Now why did you insist on seeing me?"

The General listened attentively as Chuck told him what he would like to do for Managua. He explained about the dedicated, committed Christian people who would want to come and help. He promised to bring in $500,000 worth of supplies and food and articles needed by the people.

When he finished speaking, the General slowly nodded his head and thanked Chuck for his kindness. "This matter will have to go through my Minister of Defense. He will know that you are coming."

General Somoza then summoned a photographer and instructed him to take a picture of the two of them together behind his desk, and then the interview was completed.

This meeting seemed like a true miracle for Amina and Misael and their people. From the moment Chuck was presented with the official letter that said he had President Somoza's approval to come and go as he wished, he no longer was simply Reverend Chuck Thomas. In the eyes of the nationals in Nicaragua, he was now Doctor Thomas.

Arriving home in Wichita, we did not waste a moment in getting a special newsletter out informing people of the terrible conditions in Managua. Chuck went to the Coleman Company, and they immediately gave him twenty tents and camping stoves. The Wichita newspaper ran a series of articles that brought in blankets, used clothing, and donations of medicine from various pharmacies and doctors. The news media really did us a favor. The more news they gave about the earthquake, the easier it was to find people who were willing to go with us to help.

Within two weeks, that old Convair airplane took off with people from Kansas who had said, "Here am I. Send me." The group included, among others, a lawyer, his wife and their three daughters; a stockbroker and his wife; a newspaper photographer; a farmer, a factory worker; and a postman. All united to help a desperate people in time of tragedy.

Approaching the airport in Managua, our pilot asked the tower for permission to land. The airport heretofore was one of great, impressive beauty. Now the delicately veined marble was cracked, windows were broken, and there was damage everywhere. After receiving permission to land, we were instructed to proceed off the runway and onto a ramp. There we were met by the military who insisted that all supplies were to be turned over to the government.

"On, no!" Chuck said, "I have a letter from General Somoza."

And so he did. It was a magic letter that everyone wanted to see and to keep, but he never let it out of his grasp, not even to the customs officials. From that trip on there would be no question concerning the Convair 240 that belonged to Project Partner. She always received immediate permission to land and was allowed to taxi right up to the gate where the A.M.E.N. trucks waited for the supplies. She was a special lady of the skies, and she was treated with respect.

On that first trip the work campers were taken directly from the airport to the home of Orlando and Rosemary Bell, located outside Managua city limits, where they set up their Coleman tents and went to work. They brought with them all the food they would need during their stay in Nicaragua.

The work crew was awestruck by the desolation that met them as they walked down the once bustling streets of Managua. There was nothing but rubble as far as the eye could see. It was as if the city had disappeared. It was more than they could comprehend that people were living under the piles of debris. Scattered about they would see a stick holding up a scrap of red material or a piece of white cloth.

"What does that mean?" a work camper asked.

"Someone is living under that pile and they need help," Chuck replied.

The white flag meant someone needed medical assistance. The red flag meant they were in need of food or water. They were living in places worse than hog pens, in the dirt and under any piece of loose material they could find.

One afternoon, among all the dirt and debris, John Wren, previously a business executive from Montgomery, Alabama, but now a part of Project Partner staff, found a little boy about four years old. The child huddled with his left foot terribly swollen and bandaged with a dirty piece of blue rag. His father was killed in the earthquake and his mother was out looking for food. The little boy cut his foot when he stepped on a broken bottle while searching through the ruins of his home.

When the mother returned, her face held the same blank expression that so many others wore. After the badly infected foot was treated and clean bandages applied, medication was given to relieve the boy's pain and to help fight the infection. As the mother gathered her son to her, the dullness left her eyes. Tears of gratitude flowed down her face. They were alive and they were going to make it. Someone had come. Someone cared. Jim Feiring, a stockbroker from Wichita, Kansas, smiled and handed the mother some money to buy the child a pair of shoes. She couldn't thank him enough.

That evening, as Jim finished his long day's work, he looked up to see the mother waiting for him. She held out her hand while making it plain that she had something for him. He reached his hand to her, and into his palm she dropped the left-over change. This time the smile was on her face and the tears were in Jim's eyes.

During the weeks and months after that first trip to Nicaragua, many teams boarded our plane for Managua. After we had been taking work teams for five months, Chuck felt the Lord calling him to take the choir from Gulf Coast Bible College to encourage the people. He knew that their morale was at such a dangerously low ebb and he reasoned, "What could bring them a moment's relief better than some beautiful, inspirational music?"

The choir was given permission to set up at the National Stadium with their public address equipment on the bed of a truck. This concert was presented free for all of Managua. During the months, we brought them food, medicine, and cement blocks, all for their physical needs. Now the Lord guided us to bring them music for their souls' needs.

Several months later, during one of our trips to Managua, Chuck received a request for a private audience with President Somoza. He couldn't help wondering what he might have done that could have offended the General. He went to the General's headquarters with some uneasiness.

"I suppose you wonder why I have invited you here, Reverend," the General began. "Well for one thing, I want you to meet my wife. But more than that, Reverend Thomas, I have something I wish to say to you. Spain has given us $7 million to rebuild our hospital. Mexico has given us many millions of dollars. England has sent several millions. The United States has given ..."

As General Somoza spoke, Chuck remembered when he had stood before him and with pride had said he would bring $500,000. Obviously that wasn't very much.

The General continued, "I realize that your monetary investment in our country has not been nearly so great as these I've mentioned, but I am expressing appreciation to you and your organization for the fact the you brought us people. Our people needed people. You are the only organization that brought in people, plane loads of people, to be with our Nicaraguans in their time of despair.

"I have announced a motto for our country for the next year. I have called it 'The Year of Reconstruction.' However, because of the significant contribution that you and your organization have made, I have added the words, 'and hope.' This coming year will be known as: THE YEAR OF RECON-STRUCTION—AND HOPE! Thank you, Reverend Thomas. Thank you."

Looking back we see a remarkable story. Living through it we only saw overwhelming circumstances and tremendous obstacles. God, however, gave us an opportunity to serve him in helping these people in their dire need. He guided and directed our path as we persisted in making it happen.

CHAPTER 8
CHANCES: A NEW PATH

A Gift for Ministry

We received a call one afternoon in 1973 from a man in Alabama named Ray Helms. He had a forty-seven-foot yacht he wanted to use in mission work. Having heard about Project Partner and having asked the Lord for guidance, he felt he should approach us with his dream. Chuck put down the phone and explained this amazing call to me.

"Apparently he bought it as a pleasure yacht and shortly afterward, while on its maiden voyage into Panama, he and his wife stopped and visited our missionary friends, Dean and Nina Flora." Chuck explained. "Dean apparently gave him a taste of mission that he could not forget. Dean showed him a large boat he has turned into a medical clinic, and he is using it with his ministry to the Cuna Indians.

"Later, while Ray was docked at Titusville, Florida and, in the process of refurbishing his boat, he realized that here he was pouring money into personal pleasure while there were people 'out there' who didn't have even the necessities of life. So," Chuck concluded, "he's decided to place his yacht into missions work for use as a medical clinic. He wants us to take the yacht and develop it to serve the Lord somewhere in the Caribbean."

A new chance. A new mountain to climb. Neither one of us, however, knew anything about boats. Chuck was an airplane pilot. The only time he was at sea was during World War II when he was sent to Europe on a Liberty ship. He always said he was on the water for twenty-eight days and sick for thirty.

Now what were we going to do with a forty-seven-foot yacht? Was this what the Lord wanted us to do? The Lord would have to let us know. We needed to see how it could be developed, where it would work, what it would cost, how we could staff it, and how it would accomplish bringing people to Christ as well as helping them physically.

We spent some days in prayer about this new venture. It kept becoming more interesting and exciting. As our thoughts reviewed myriads of questions, we became sure that this was what the Lord wanted us to do.

One of the first things we had to do was to decide where a medical boat was most needed. My mind went back to the baby that fell in the fire in La Esperanza, Guatemala when we were there on a work camp. Dr. Jim Wray and his wife, Margaret, were with us on that trip so we opened a temporary clinic during our time there. A neighbor had brought the child as the mother felt there was no hope and the father was working a couple of hundred miles away on the Pacific coast. This child had burns over 75 percent of his body as well as appearing malnourished and needing urgent care. Dr. Wray felt we needed to get him to the nearest hospital which was in the city of Quezaltenango, about twenty-five miles away. We had seen not only this child but many others that needed medical attention. We knew Guatemala had a dire need for medical care. We did not, however, know anything about the rivers or ports for the boat. So the next step up this mountain was to check out the area, the possibilities, and the need.

We were working in Guatemala with Isai Calderon and with other pastors and leaders in Guatemala City for three years by this time, so we had some contacts. Because we had been taking workcamp teams there in our airplane, we felt we knew the area pretty well. We decided that would be a good place to start.

Talking with Isai, Chuck chose Lake Izabal and the Rio Dulce on the East Coast as the best place for our maiden voyage. Many unreached tribal people lived in that area with only one hospital. Chuck would have to go to Guatemala to check out the river and the lake, and to see if it could handle a boat. That is how Chuck got lost in the jungle along the Rio Dulce (sweet river).

Our Guide in the Jungle

When he arrived in Livingston, Chuck was already tired from the long, bone-wearying journey to get to Guatemala. As he flew he was reliving the past few days and thinking of Ray and Betty Helms back in Titusville, Florida. This couple was ready to donate the "Sea Angel" for her first medical-Gospel voyage, and they were awaiting Chuck's direction. He'd find the energy somehow to take the next step.

Chuck flew from Wichita into Guatemala City, and after securing the services of a Mission Aviation Fellowship pilot, they flew over eastern Guatemala.

"Looks like a patchwork quilt down there, doesn't it?" Chuck commented. "The tiny plots of cultivated crops and small clustered huts surrounded by the dark green of the jungle always look so formidable, so impenetrable somehow."

"Except, of course, by the rivers," responded Jim, the pilot.

"The rivers look almost like a blue ribbon carelessly discarded. Hey! Look down there! That's beautiful! Swing around that way again," Chuck shouted over the noise of the engine.

"That's the Rio Dulce. She's surely beautiful from up here," said Jim.

"Seems to be a few villages along her, too. Well, let's get back and see what we can find out," Chuck added.

"You haven't exactly picked an easily accessible area, sir," said Jim.

"There'll be a way, there always is when the Lord is guiding you," Chuck assured himself under his breath.

Back in Guatemala City, needing to know whether Sea Angel could navigate the Rio Dulce and whether people along the river needed our help, Chuck located an anthropologist, Jose Ramero, to guide him in finding that beautiful river. They began by taking a bus two hundred miles to Puerto Barrios. From there on, all travel had to be done by ferry and cayuca or canoe. It was twenty-five miles by ferry to the small settlement of Livingston at the mouth of the river.

When he arrived in Livingston, Chuck and his guide had to head up the river by cayuca to find the answers to his questions. Chuck was told that the village he was heading for was at least ten miles up the river. He made arrangements with the only hotelkeeper in Livingston to keep his belongings until his return, grabbed his raincoat, and hurried off to join his guide.

The cayuca trip began smoothly; however, typical of that part of the world, the peace and quiet of a beautiful day were shortly interrupted by a breeze and then drops of rain. Chuck noticed that towering thunderheads were gathering at an alarming rate. He slipped into his raincoat just before the rain became serious. Running his hands in his pockets, he came across the bag of Tootsie Rolls I sent along with him. That was one of his favorite candies, and it always made a good snack to take along on a trip.

Around the next bend in the river, his guide headed the cayuca toward a village that had been shielded from their view. Chuck scrambled out of the cayuca, lowering his head against the driving rain, and headed toward the cluster of huts. As the storm intensified, Chuck tried to talk to some of the Indians who were scurrying around, only to find out that they didn't speak Spanish or English but the ancient language of Kekchi. His guide disappeared among the huts of the village after telling Chuck that he found a lady friend there.

It wasn't long before Chuck saw that some of the Indians were packing up their belongings and hurrying past him on the path. They all seemed headed in one direction, the high country.

Not at all sure what he should do, Chuck followed along and soon found himself walking beside an old man carrying on his back a chair stacked precariously with what seemed to be all his personal possessions. They smiled and nodded at each other and hurriedly walked on together.

The rain intensified and ran in rivulets down his face, then underneath his collar and soaking his clothes. His trouser legs were wet and his feet sloshed in his shoes with each step. "This is more than just a jungle afternoon rain," he thought. As the wind direction abruptly changed, realization set in and concern quickly possessed him. Being a pilot and having studied atmospheric pressure and weather conditions, he knew that this was going to be a bad storm. He also remembered how the winds changed in the eye of a storm like this as it intensified.

On and on the Indians hurried, higher and higher, trying their hardest to escape the torrents of rain. Chuck knew that the higher they went the more intense the winds would become, so he began frantically trying to change their direction.

"Wait! *Espere! Espere!*" he shouted to no avail. They looked at him, this white man, a full head and a half taller than any of them, but they couldn't understand him and so they hurried on.

"Stop! *Pare! Pare!*" Chuck shouted. He knew they were going the wrong way. He reached out and took his elderly companion by the elbow and then, just as quickly, reached into his pocket and took out a Tootsie Roll. "*Aqui.* See?" The old man stopped walking and tasted the chocolate. Chuck handed out more Tootsie Rolls to anyone who would listen. They liked the candy and began to accept him as they moved along.

They came to a "Y" in the road and in order to keep the wind at their backs, they took the right-hand fork.

"*Pare!* Stop!" Chuck yelled desperately. He knew that this was a low-pressure system with the wind blowing counterclockwise. To escape the fullness of the raging storm they would have to first walk into the wind.

By sign language and Tootsie Rolls, Chuck got them to follow him and stay on the leeward side of the storm. The Indians realized that as long as they followed him, they were out of the stinging, biting, raging storm. This wasn't easy. There were times when his energy was gone and he would have to stop and rest. Those who walked with him showed their concern for him and when he stopped, they too stopped and waited. They continued, one foot wearily placed in front of the other again and again until they found a place where the winds had stopped, staying there to wait out the storm.

For centuries the Indians have placed their special altars of worship high atop the mountains, huge altars of stone covered with pine needles. In times of trouble, so they have been taught, the gods are angry and must be appeased by sacrifices. Now that the storm was over, they seemed compelled to move onward, upward to their sacred ground.

Tired and aching, Chuck knew he must not continue upward. His task lay back in the village. And so, after much gesturing and embracing, nodding and smiling, they parted and he began his trek back down the mountain.

First thing I have to do, Chuck thought as he became suddenly aware of his aloneness, is to get to the river. Whoever said that the longest journey is begun by taking the first step forgot to say in just which direction that first step should be taken.

His feet and legs ached, and sometimes it was difficult to follow the narrow path. Often it was impossible to tell whether it was going up or down, or merely around in circles. The faint paths that crisscrossed the heavy jungle growth, appeared well traveled, which only added to his already confused state. The jungle surrounded him with its heavy wall of dark green, forbidding growth. And as night suddenly and totally settled in, his confusion turned to fear.

Wearily he sat down on a fallen tree trunk and found another Tootsie Roll for his supper. He tried to rest by leaning back against a tree branch. *Maybe I'll spend the night here,* he thought as he tried to shut his eyes. Discomfort and fear surrounded him. He knew something about the deadly snakes in these jungles. He could not stay there, so he spent the rest of the night as he had spent the day, stumbling on, to what, he was not at all sure.

Though the night was terrifying, he kept reminding himself that he was okay and it would pass. His mind also reminded him that he had hundreds of dollars in his money belt, money enough to buy whatever he needed, money to buy a great meal and a clean wonderful bed. It was worthless there. The only thing of value that he had now was his plastic bag of Tootsie Rolls.

The night that came too swiftly, without notice, gave signs of lifting. The birds began a tentative talking that grew into shrill calls as they heralded the start of day. Time ceased to exist in normal, common denominators and became as distorted as the path ahead. By day he reminded himself to travel eastward. He knew he had to follow the water down and kept plodding along until finally he was ankle deep in the swamp. Each step was traumatic, not knowing how deep the next would be and knowing that there were snakes in these swamps.

The second night he stumbled on a large rock, large enough that he climbed upon its smooth surface and pressed his aching tired form down for a bit of sleep. At long last, during a daylight period, along the path came a small group of natives, all carrying machetes.

"Habla español?" Chuck cried out as he stumbled towards them. They stared at him, this haggard, worn white man. But then they put their heads down and pushed past him, hurrying on.

On and on he plodded. Gradually the paths changed; they seemed more distinct. He started taking the ones that seemed to be most traveled, always heading eastward. Finally he began coming across other small groups of natives walking the paths.

"Habla español?"

Sometimes they would hesitate, looking him over. They were polite. Even when they did not understand him, they would stand and listen. Fearfully, they would accept the Tootsie Rolls he offered, watch him eat one first, eat theirs, and then head on.

He stumbled on for hours more until he wearily raised his eyes and saw a grotto. Wow! He stopped at the grotto. There was a small statue of the Virgin and an area where the dark green jungle vines and growth had been beaten back to accommodate it. With relief surging through him, he knew that where a grotto like this is, a Catholic priest could be nearby.

With the next group of Indians, he tried again.

"*Donde esta Livingston? Donde esta la iglesia* (where is the church)?"

The group seemed to understand, pointing in some direction or other before leaving him standing there.

The path became more traveled. He stumbled on, eventually finding a group of huts. Chuck hurriedly approached the one that looked to be the most open, the most inviting. Inside he could see there were children and chickens and one old woman.

Chuck motioned to the old woman to come outside. The children came out cautiously and she finally followed. He handed each a Tootsie Roll, unwrapping one for himself to show them they could eat it.

He tried his questions again. "*Donde esta la iglesia?*" They seemed to understand, and with sign language pointed out one specific path as they held out their hands for more Tootsie Rolls.

In sign language he attempted to ask them, "How far?"

In sign language they conveyed, "A long, long way."

With renewed energy, Chuck moved on, nursing the hope within him that perhaps there was an end to this nightmare. Finally, in the distance, he could see the jungle giving way to small fields of corn. Closer and closer he came to them until he could have reached out and pulled the ears from the stalks. Rising before him like a mirage was a small Catholic Church, and beyond that, a small town.

Chuck had found the Catholic church and the priest, Father Juan, who even spoke English. Chuck told him the whole story. Taking him into a small room in the back, the priest showed him his ham radio. Praise the Lord! There was now a way for Chuck to communicate with the world.

Of course, there had been great concern for the missing Chuck back in Wichita. The news of the terrible storm in Guatemala and Honduras had made the front page of the papers. I knew he was in that area and he did not call in as he was supposed to three days earlier. I had called the national leader, Isai Calderon, but he didn't know where Chuck was either. My next call was to the State Department, asking for the

Guatemala Desk. The man at that Desk knew of the storm but had no knowledge of Chuck or a lost American. However, they told me to call back in twenty-four hours if I did not hear from him and they would send a team in to search for him.

Then I called Chester Lemmond, one of our work camp team leaders. After hearing my story he reassured me, saying, "Okay Donna, I'll go and see what I can find out. I'll find him." We didn't have to wait twenty-four hours and Chester didn't have to go.

My phone rang at home. "You don't know me. I live in Georgia. I'm a ham radio operator and I have a radio message to patch through to you. Do you know how a radio patch works? Are you ready? I believe it is a Father Thomas, Ma'am. It's a radio dispatch from a Catholic Church near Livingston, Guatemala."

"Honey, I'm fine. I know you've been worried and it has been really rough but the Lord has brought me through. He's been my guide in this jungle. I'm coming home. In the morning I'll get to Livingston and catch a bus to Guatemala City. I should be able to get a plane from there the next morning and I'll call you from New Orleans."

Washed and fed and filled with a feeling of exhilaration plus relief, Chuck bid his fellow "man of the cloth" goodbye, promising to bring him supplies when Sea Angel arrived in this area in about two months. This was a relationship that was now precious.

Within a short while, seated before the port captain, Chuck told the story of Sea Angel and what they wished to do for his people if he could give them permission to navigate the waters of the Rio Dulce. As Chuck rose to leave with the written permission in his hand, the port captain stopped him.

"Pardon me, *señor,* for staring at you, but you are so tall. Perhaps you have been in the jungle walking these last few days? During the storm?

"Well, yes I have. Why do you ask?"

"This accounts for the reports I have been receiving. The Indians say there was a tall white man out there in the midst of the storm. They are saying, 'God walked the jungle during the storm.' "

"God?"

"*Si:* God. They say they know it was God, for during the storm where he walked, where he led them, there was no wind."

CHAPTER 9

STEWARDSHIP: GIVING IT AWAY

Jorge Eduardo Murillo was the first boy in our Agape child sponsorship program in Costa Rica. He was ten-years-old as he stood there to have his picture taken, looking proud and happy as he held the numbers we assigned to him for our system of accounting: 000001. A small church in Chattanooga, Tennessee was willing to sponsor this boy. With their monthly support the Agape director in Costa Rica, Amina Lopez, was able to see that Jorge had an education, adequate food, and spiritual guidance. It paid off. That church in Tennessee invested a total of $2,700 in Jorge over nine years. He is now a pastor in Grecia, Costa Rica. After high school, he went on to complete his ministerial training and committed his life to serving the Lord as a minister. Giving produces results.

Investments

In the mid-70s we met Dr. Larry Poland, a young man working with Campus Crusade for Christ. He was overseeing the missions program, World Thrust, in Kansas City. Chuck and I knew that we needed some help in developing Project Partner more effectively, but we didn't know where any help was available. Something prompted us to drive the two hundred miles to Kansas City to see what World Thrust could mean to us.

Larry Poland listened intently to what we had to say, felt our commitment to expanding the ministry, and saw how he could help us. Getting the approval of Dr. Bill Bright, the president and founder of Campus Crusade, he invited us and our work-camp director, Claude Ferguson, to come to Campus Crusade's headquarters in Arrowhead Springs, California. We were their guests for ten days during which they shared with us how their organization functioned. And they would advise us on ours.

I remember vividly the day Larry took us to an upstairs room at their headquarters and sat us down before a blackboard. He wanted to write our purpose statement down as we shared it with him. The problem was that we never really took the time to clearly articulate it. Sounds easy now, but it was difficult then. With Larry's help, we worked on the purpose, plans, functions, and goals, of each of our programs and how they could be enhanced and developed. At this point in time we had twenty-five staff members.

Larry and Dr. Bright invested about two weeks of their time in us plus the cost of our being there. They had no way of knowing how God would use us in the future, but they gave of themselves to us in faith and it turned out to be extremely valuable for our ministry and for our part in extending the Kingdom of God.

It was from their investment, their example, that we developed our operating principles, including our plan for "giving everything away." We were never interested in building a name for Project Partner. Our purpose was always to build the Kingdom of God by investing in others and empowering them. We discovered during the years that "you never lose what you give away."

A Gift to Us

We had much to learn about giving from the nationals, too. Some Guatemalan Indians taught us a lesson we would never forget. We were in the village of Durazno, up in the mountains but not too far from the Guatemala City airport. We were constructing a church building in that area, in a nearby village. The evening before our trip back home, our team had a special service with this neighboring village. Even though we were not working for them, they wanted to host us that evening. There were pine needles spread over the floor of their little church, which were to give a pungent smell as their traditional sign of welcome. The Indian women had food ready to feed our group to express their appreciation for our help in their country. They graciously presented each one in our group a plate of hot and sweet tamales they had made with loving care.

The church was packed full that evening and people were crowding around outside the windows as well. As was their custom, the men sat on one side of the church and the women and children on the other. They sang songs of worship and we tried to join in but it was more interesting to listen. About twenty minutes into the service, I heard the leader say in Spanish that an offering would be taken. Not unusual. He went on to say, however, that it was for the guests. That was us. These poor village farmers, were going to take an offering for us. I couldn't believe it. This had never happened before. We were the ones with money in our pockets, not these people.

These villagers knew that our airplane took a lot of gasoline, so they wanted to help us pay for it. As the musician played his two-string instrument, two of their people passed through the congregation, extending a long stick with a bag on the end of it down each row to their own people. The ushers brought the bags to the front and dumped the offering into the hands of the pastor. As Chuck received this offering from the pastor, he was overwhelmed and didn't know how to respond. He graciously accepted their gift. Then he bowed his head in prayer to thank the Lord for people like this who cared so much for us strangers from the United States and who made this effort to express their love.

In our room that night, we spread their offering out on the bed. There it was, in small coins and crumpled notes. It came to $5.60. That doesn't sound like much but it was a lot from these people. A farmer's daily wage was around eighty cents a day. Multiply that by seven for a week's income and it comes to $5.60. Then too, the Bible tells that that seven is the perfect number. This was indeed a generous and loving gift, a sacrificial amount, their perfect gift.

We pondered what we could do with the $5.60. Our gasoline costs on a trip like this were around $2,500. What difference would $5.60 make? Chuck quickly decided. He said they gave it for gasoline, and it was going to go for gasoline, and so it did.

Our plane was parked on the tarmac not far from the front fence. As we gathered our team for departure the next morning, we saw that a good many of those village people had walked down the mountain to see us off. There they were leaning against the chain link fence, waving and shouting, "Adios, amigos." We all automatically went to the fence to shake hands and say our good-byes. The fence wouldn't allow us to give them one of those Latin American hugs before climbing aboard our plane. Chuck always said that the plane took off better than ever that day because of the fuel that they helped us buy.

Those Guatemalans taught us a lesson on giving that day which we really needed. We started our work in their country by purchasing some land and building a medical clinic on Lake Izabal. We were to see the needs and to give our offerings. From that time on, Project Partner did not own anything in a foreign country. It made more sense to give it all away and to do so sacrificially, as those Guatemalan farmers did that day.

Sea Angel, Our Medical Boat

Having a medical boat in Central America was one thing. Finding the crew and staff for it was something else. However, as word got out about this boat, God always provided just the right people to serve him in this way, people who wanted to be good stewards of their life.

The first Captain was Vernon Allison. He knew all about boating even though he was a young student at Warner Southern College in Florida. Vernon, then known as Bunky, took a couple of semesters off to work with us. Gladys Smith, a nurse from Muncie, Indiana, volunteered, too. Vic and Betty

Demarest knew how to handle a boat and followed Vernon when he went back to college. Hugo Moriera was a young man in Wichita from Uruguay who went on board as a pastor and started some churches in Guatemala. His passion for the Lord and his knowledge of Spanish was just what was needed.

As we grew to understand the culture in Guatemala, we saw how important it was to be sensitive to the needs and to be able to share time, skills, and compassion as well as monetary supplies. Life and money had different values in the countries of Central America. Gladys, our first Sea Angel nurse out on Lake Izabal in Guatemala, was always relating stories along these lines. There were no hospitals close to where Sea Angel was located. And there were none like those to which we were accustomed. Gladys explained, "If a child is taken to the hospital, he is left there alone. Someone has to be found to take milk in to him, or else he is given none. The hospital will provide only pureed beans and rice.

"Then," Gladys continued, "the only way his family has of knowing whether the patient has recovered and is going to be released from the hospital, or perhaps has died, is by listening to the local radio. The radio broadcasts daily who is well enough to be released and who has died. Guatemala is only about the size of Tennessee and there are more than 7 million inhabitants. One million children are unable to attend school, more than one million never have enough food, and 80 percent of the children suffer from malnutrition. There just isn't a very high premium on human life. Sometimes they suffer from disease or accidents that we have never heard of."

Dr. Bob Yager, an oral surgeon from Charles City, Iowa, heard about our medical missions boat, Sea Angel, and became interested in this ministry. After much inquiry, arrangements were made for him to meet Chuck in Guatemala at the remote airstrip close to Lake Izabal.

As Dr. Yager and the pilot who was hired to fly him in from Guatemala City were flying over the Rio Dulce, the pilot called out, "Look over there—far to your right. That's where you're headed."

"How beautiful she is," thought Dr. Yager as he gazed down at the Sea Angel. It appeared like some fragile, regal, white bird floating on a shimmering crystal ribbon and surrounded by every shade of green imaginable.

When the plane had landed and its passenger was left standing on the ground, the man running toward him called out, "Dr. Yager? I'm Chuck Thomas." Together they hurried across the field to the river, and into the cayuca, which Chuck expertly headed toward the Sea Angel situated a few miles away at anchor. When they came to her, Chuck pulled the cayuca alongside and secured it. Gladys, our nurse who was waiting topside for them, called out, "I'm so glad to see you." After climbing the ladder to the deck, Chuck introduced Gladys to Dr. Yager.

"I'm especially happy to see you, Doctor," said Gladys. "At the moment we have a young boy on board who is in need of help. A short while ago a cayuca came out to us. It's tied to the back and the boy's father refuses to come on board. He's just sitting there waiting in the cayuca. The boy is young, perhaps seven years old but very small for his age, really just a bit of a wisp. In my opinion, he is suffering from parasites. There is a large knot on his head."

"Worms?" Dr. Yager questioned.

"There is a lot of that here," she continued. It's one of our greatest problems. Doctor, I need you to operate on him."

"Gladys, Reverend Thomas neglected to tell you that I am not a medical doctor. I am a dentist, an oral surgeon," Dr. Yager asserted.

"Doctor, if you don't operate, I will have to and I'm definitely not any kind of surgeon," she replied.

"But we haven't the proper facilities or equipment. I can't do that," he responded.

"Come see him," Gladys insisted. The doctor followed her, in spite of his misgivings.

Sitting on deck in a dental chair that had been donated was a small, dark-skinned, dark-haired, dark-eyed little boy not much larger than a whisper. On his head was a knot as large as a man's fist.

"Dr. Yager, please," Gladys pleaded again.

"Well, Reverend," the words came slowly while the man painstakingly accepted the difficult task with apprehension. "You must really pray for us."

Chuck responded, "I'll do that."

Standing there on the open deck, with the Rio Dulce tapping at the Angel's hull, Chuck began to talk to God. "Lord, you know we're here because you brought us here. These are unsanitary conditions and we don't have what is needed. But we're here because we feel that you want us to be here, and Lord, we're depending on you."

Gladys went below and returned with everything she thought Dr. Yager might need for the operation.

"Nurse, do we have anything to use for a local anesthetic?"

"No, Doctor, nothing."

"Woman, what do you expect this little fellow to do while I'm operating?"

"Doctor, I'll hold him," Gladys said softly.

Turning away from her, the doctor methodically arranged the tray of sutures, needles, antiseptic, sponges, and scalpels in the fashion that would aid him the most effectively. This most assuredly was not going to be easy. Operating in the open air, with the assistance of one nurse and one preacher, in an operating theater that was moving about on water, and with no anesthetic. Impossible!

While the doctor was getting ready, Gladys went back to the father sitting in the cayuca and asked him if he would come and hold his son while they operated. He refused.

When everything was made as ready as possible, Gladys took the child's hands in hers and Chuck gently placed his hands on the boy's tiny, thin shoulders.

"Ready, Doctor?"

"Ready."

Dr. Yager closed his eyes for a second and sighed deeply. Nothing up to now had prepared him for anything like this.

Then, opening his eyes and looking at nothing except the problem before him, he picked up a razor from the tray and began shaving the boy's head. The child did not move. Laying the razor back on the tray, he swabbed the shaved area with antiseptic. Then, with thin, sensitive, strong fingers he picked up the scalpel.

Chuck and Gladys watched as the silver colored, stainless steel blade traveled across the swollen lump, leaving a thin red line which widened suddenly. Grabbing gauze sponges, they quickly and expertly mopped away the fluids that alternately gushed and trickled from the incision. Intently and precisely Dr. Yager concentrated on what he was doing. Using extreme care, he was able to extract the worm and larvae responsible for the abnormal growth.

After the area was cleaned and the suturing complete, Dr. Yager stepped back and breathed deeply. Then, and only then, he allowed himself truly to look at the child. A sudden realization swept over him. The boy never moved. He did not whimper and he did not cry, not one small tear. "I can't believe it," he thought. "If I hadn't seen it, I wouldn't believe it."

Bob and Chuck cleaned up the area and washed their hands. Gladys gave the boy pills for infection. Gently she helped him to his feet and together they started walking towards the cayuca, but suddenly the boy stopped. Slowly he walked the few short steps back to where Dr. Yager stood, put his small, dirty hand into his pocket, and took out a Guatemalan dime, wordlessly handing it to Dr. Yager.

Overcome with emotion, the doctor turned the grimy coin over in the palm of his hand, the muscles of his jaw contracting, and with a smile that tears threatened to erase, he placed the dime back in the child's pocket.

"Doctor," Chuck said, clearing his throat. "Tell the little boy why you came here."

"I'm a doctor," he began. "I love the Lord Jesus. If my little boy were sick, I would hope someone would help him. The Lord sent me here to help you. He loves us and I love you. That's why I am here."

With Gladys interpreting, the boy listened to those words. Later, the boy told his father, the father told his brother, the brother told his neighbor, and the neighbor told his neighbor. Because of the words the little boy heard that day, people started coming to Sea Angel for healing of their bodies and their souls.

After supper that evening, Chuck came topside and joined Gladys and Dr. Yager as they sat relaxing from the exhausting day.

"Everything is so different here," Bob Yager said. "It's almost like being in another world."

"It is another world, and it takes some getting used to. This is a part of the 'third world' and it's totally unlike the world from which you come," Gladys responded.

"Tell me, Gladys, if I hadn't been here today to operate on that little boy, just what would you have done?"

"I believe I answered that earlier. I would have done it myself," she replied without hesitation. "Don't look so skeptical. I know that in the United States nurses don't cut and suture. And, to tell you the truth, a few short years ago, it simply wouldn't have entered my mind to attempt such a thing. But, Doctor, circumstances here make things different."

"Just suppose for a moment that you are a trained nurse. Suppose that you have seen hundreds of children and adults with similar problems and that you have watched while many different MDs have performed this procedure. Now, Doctor, just suppose that standing before you is a child who will die if this procedure is not done ... and there is no physician within hundreds of miles and no time or means to transport him. Then, doctor, tell me what would you do?"

"No question, I'd excise the thing."

"And so would I," Gladys added.

The doctor turned toward Chuck, "Reverend," he said, "what is the biggest need here?"

After a few seconds of contemplation, Chuck thoughtfully replied, "Not enough."

"Not enough what?"

"Everything! Not enough doctors. Not enough medicines. Not enough adequate transportation, or money, or ways of communication. Not enough knowledge, not enough time, simply not enough.

"Do you know," Chuck continued, "there are times when these decks are full of people waiting for help? Perhaps we should prepare you for what may happen tomorrow. Starting early, the cayucas will swarm about and attach themselves to the Sea Angel. Then the decks will be filled with sixty or so sick and ailing. I have seen times when we were anchored on Lake Izabal that the people stayed here far into the time when the strong winds made it dangerous for the cayucas to be out there. But they stayed because they needed help.

"Why, do you know that in a month's time, Gladys will see over four-hundred patients?" Chuck wanted him to know the extent of the challenge we were facing on our hospital/Gospel ship.

"That's a lot of patients." Dr. Yager exclaimed.

"Yes, it is. And along with not enough hands and medication, the price of fuel goes up constantly. It takes upward of three hundred gallons a month for this Angel. And in addition there's the cost of insurance, food for the crew, and we have to hire a cook and a boatman. Something most people don't think about is the cost of bandages alone. It is unbelievable.

"Then there's finding someone capable of serving as captain and doctors and nurses who are dedicated, skilled, and willing to donate their services for a given period of time like you have. All of that takes lots of time and money."

"It seems like an impossible task," Dr. Yager responded. "What special types of medical problems do you encounter?"

"Well, if it's a medical problem in the jungle, eventually, we see they will come to us, whatever it is," said Gladys. "We run into all kinds of infections, some we don't even have names for. There are always machete cuts, insect bites, and snakebites. It seems there are poisonous snakes everywhere."

"Not long ago," Chuck interrupted, "a group of men were out working and a marvelous fellow, treasurer of the church we built here, turned over a banana leaf and a snake bit him."

"And," Gladys continued the story, "we had no serum. He knew he would die. There was no way to get help for him soon enough to do any good."

"He just accepted it as inevitable," Chuck added. "He didn't fight it, or lament, he just accepted it."

"But, how could he?" Bob asked incredulously.

"Because," Gladys told him, "these people are raised knowing the probability of snakebites and knowing there is no available help. He knew what was happening, and he accepted it. There was no other way."

"What *did* happen?"

"Gladys held him in her arms and with a smile on his lips, he said his 'good-byes' and died," Chuck answered.

Chuck related another encounter, the time when a father came to a clinic in Bolivia carrying his son who was very ill and likely to die without help. "The father was asked by the clinic worker to pay fifty-five cents for his son's medicine. The man took some coins from his pocket, counted them, and when he saw that he had only seventy-five cents, without any hesitation at all, he said, 'No, never mind,' and turned to leave.

"The clinic worker called after him, 'Wait. He can stay for thirty cents.'

"But the father said, 'No. There are four children at home and I will have another child next year. No, I cannot pay the thirty cents. I can buy a casket for twenty-five cents.' And before anyone could stop him, he was out the door and disappeared with his son into the crowd. These are the experiences that cause people like Gladys to give their all to the Lord."

There was a long pause. The only sound was the water slapping against the ship's hull.

"I don't know how you can stand it."

"It's all part of being here," said Gladys.

There was quiet for a little while until Gladys continued. "Some of our time is spent in trying to teach, to educate these people. We try to teach the local midwives to use more sterile techniques with women in labor. The government sends in literature, and we try to distribute it and explain it. The regret is that, when there is a problem, usually we are not sent for until it is too late."

In the gathering silence, Dr. Yager cleared his throat and turned to face Gladys. "Tell me, Gladys, just why are you here? What brought you here?"

"Because I cannot forget what God expects of us. We are our brother's keeper."

The Joy of Giving

Chuck recalls an encounter at the airport in Managua during their Revolution that put stewardship in yet another perspective. As he was sitting there waiting to board his flight to come home, the young Nicaraguan man next to him initiated a conversation in English. Chuck found out he was a communist and very supportive of the Cuban military forces that were currently in Nicaragua. This young man asked Chuck why he was in Managua. This gave Chuck the opportunity to tell about how we were building churches and schools to help the Nicaraguan Christians.

With this the young man jumped to his feet and started yelling. "You Christians," he said, " you are everywhere. You are everywhere I go. There are Christians behind every tree and behind every rock. I just can't get away from you Christians."

That was a new viewpoint, and one Chuck was happy to tell us when he got home. He only wished that it were true.

As this missions and ministry philosophy of Project Partner developed, I began to realize that an even greater ministry could develop if we could devise a way to further empower the nationals we were working with. Truly, we could help to make this Nicaraguan's statement come true—that Christians would be everywhere. The idea was born that we could help them establish their own mission agency in the United States. We could help them form their own corporation, get the IRS nonprofit status, and put them in control of their future here. So we incorporated Enrique Cepeda's Mexican ministry as *Doulos International Ministries,* Andrei Bondarenko's Russian ministry as *Christian Tent Ministries,* and Samuel Stephen's India ministry as *India Gospel League, North America.* In the bylaws, for example, it states that the president of *Doulos International Ministries* in Mexico is the president of *Doulos International Ministries* in the United States. The same is true for the others. It is important to me that they be in control of their future rather than be in a position to be used as a pawn for enterprising North Americans. I discovered that this very scenario happened to others in the past, and so I sought to protect our nationals' futures through this bold new move.

At this point I also chose to make a major change in the financial structure of Project Partner. We always operated with the policy that 84 percent of every dollar donated to the ministry went to the national leaders and Project Partner retained 16 percent for overhead. I was proud of that percentage. However, I felt it was time for a change of policy to enable 100 percent of the funds designated for a ministry to go directly into that ministry. That step of faith was a bit frightening, but I believed the Lord would supply our need. In the process, we downsized Project Partner to make it more efficient and began raising the money for its operation separately. So far, so good. The Lord continues to supply and we were certainly full of joy to give to the work of the nationals in this way.

The Lord provides. I also discovered about this time that I needed to be willing to put my own money into the ministry as well to make things happen. We would never have that bus if we waited for someone else to supply the money. We started it with personal funds, signed a personal note, and then the Lord provided. The same thing happened with the airplane. We would never have the airplane if we waited for someone else. We stepped out first and then the Lord provided. After we take the first step, then sometimes there comes along a donor with a big heart who can really help.

That's what happened with the two printing presses. These are totally different situations but they show how the Lord provides as God's people respond.

At our office in Ohio we had an old ABDick press. We bought it used, had depended on it for years, and it was on its last legs. We really needed something better. Checking the possibilities and prices, I ran into a big problem. All of them were too expensive. We didn't have any funds to get anything better. I don't suppose any missions agency ever does. As our press kept breaking down and limping along, we were making it a matter of prayer with our staff. It wasn't long before this need found a position in our prayer letter that went out to our prayer partners.

Then a call came to the office. Chauncey Dean, a man very interested in Project Partner, inquired what this need of a press was all about. In a few days, I was on my way to his office with a brochure explaining the best price I had been able to find in our area. That man believed in us and chose to invest financially in providing a new press for us. It was one of those times when the Lord provides through someone willing to contribute personal money for the furtherance of the Gospel.

The second printing press story relates to a press in Salem, India, that produces volumes of materials for evangelism, discipleship, and church growth in several languages, providing a tremendous help to the India Gospel League. The ministry got its new press because Phama Wickizer went with us on an EyeWitness crusade to India. She, as well as the entire group, was intrigued with all the different facets of the ministry in India. She certainly loved those children's programs. Feeding the lepers reached her heart as it always does mine. Then I showed her Samuel Stephen's printing department.

There it was. The old press was operating by inserting one piece of paper, pulling the plate down, pressing it hard, lifting it up, taking out the paper, and starting the whole process over again. Phama's husband had been the owner of a large printing establishment in Shelbyville, Indiana, before his death, so Phama knew a lot about the printing business. She knew that this method of printing for the India Gospel League had to be changed. She asked me how much would it take to replace that ancient model.

Phama made a commitment to buy a new press. Her plans were to work it out so that in about a year she would have the funds for it. Then her mind was quickly changed. She was in her eighties, and after she had been home from the EyeWitness trip for about two weeks, she suffered a heart attack. Fortunately she had excellent and immediate medical care, but as she was lying there in the hospital room, she started to panic. She knew if she died then, Samuel would not get his printing press. Calling in her attorney, she proceeded to make the arrangements to provide the funds immediately. Today, there is a beautiful four-color press rolling out materials for the people in India that they may be brought into a wonderful relationship with the Savior. Here, was one who chose to invest in the Kingdom.

There have been many over the years who have helped Project Partner and our national leaders by their investments. I cannot forget others who, although living solely on social security, have sent a contribution month after month to serve the Lord's work. Some of these gifts have never been more than five dollars, but as I have told the staff, we are responsible to see to it that those gifts of love and sacrifice do the most they can for the Kingdom of God. We want to be faithful to those who trust us with the Lord's money in furthering his Gospel to those remote areas of the world.

I look in my purse and see my funds. The question jumps at me, "Am I doing the best that I can with my own money?" In the light of eternity, it would be a pity to build up a huge estate of "things" to be disposed of at death when an investment in ministry would have eternal results.

You never lose what you give away, because investing your time, like Bill Bright did, and investing your funds for "gas" as the Indians did, and investing your talents to "be your brother's keeper" as Gladys did, and investing "100 percent" as Project Partner did brings great rewards both here and in eternity. Besides, there is real joy in giving.

CHAPTER 10
CRUCIFIXION: CHOOSE THE LORD'S RESPONSE

On January 7, 1992, Chuck was diagnosed with stomach cancer. We didn't know what all that meant, but the word *cancer* struck terror in our hearts. The doctors said it was incurable, inoperable, and he would only live a short time, maybe three to six months. That was impossible to comprehend.

Chuck was a great husband and we enjoyed a terrific marriage. I believed all marriages lasted "forever after," not realizing there is an end as suggested in "till death do us part." Chuck was well for five years since the Lord had healed him of his heart trouble and his earlier brush with death. He appeared to be in great health and we were having a wonderful time together with dreams and plans for the future.

Just in June of 1991 he had taken a medical team to Peru. It was a rugged trip up in those steep Andes Mountains. They were in remote villages, eating strange food, and staying in primitive facilities. When he came home he told me that he didn't feel good and that his stomach was really upset, but we thought it was because of the difficulties of the trip. He'd get better soon.

In August Chuck again had stomach problems. Since he was working with so many doctors now at the University Hospital in Cincinnati, he chose to go there and see one of his friends. Dr. Jeannie Kreckeler had gone to China with him and was a part of his volunteer medical team. She put him through some tests but there didn't seem to be any problem that they could find.

That fall we had plans to go to Russia to meet with our new national leader. Andrei Bondarenko was producing tremendous results with a tent ministry and he seemed to fit into our purpose and goals quite well. The next step was to go to his country, see firsthand what was happening, and meet his team. Chuck and I enjoyed the time together and the experience of seeing Andrei's work and meeting his team. We rode the Orient Express, met some Christian leaders in St. Petersburg, flew in Russian airplanes, explored Moscow, visited and spoke about Christ in a Russian prison, and got to know Andrei very well on his own turf. His family was a delight. His ministry teams were doing a great job. He appeared to have a tremendous future for the Kingdom of God. For the moment, we'd forgotten about the stomach problems.

December came and I needed to be in Florida. There were four churches that requested help, so Chuck and I went down there for a week. Some of our time was spent meeting with those churches, but some of it was just the two of us vacationing together. Life was good, and we were looking forward to the upcoming holidays.

Christmas with our kids was wonderful. It can't get any better than having your family all together. We always made Christmas a wonderful celebration and this year was no exception. Two new grandchildren that year made everything extra special.

Facing Problems

Then it was January. We laid out plans for 1992. The first thing for me was to take an EyeWitness team of twelve to India to see what Samuel Stephens was doing. Chuck surprised me by telling me that it was time to check out his stomach again. The pain seemed to be coming back and getting worse.

It was Monday night when Chuck came home from having a MRI at the hospital in Cincinnati. I was packing my bags to leave the next day to take the group to India for two weeks.

"Honey, you'd better sit down. I've got bad news today with my tests," Chuck hesitated, then went on. "They found stomach cancer and they tell me it is incurable. They tell me that this is fast moving and I don't have very long to live."

"Wait a minute. What are you saying? Slow down, I can't believe this." I collapsed in my chair. "Stomach cancer? And you are going to die? Oh, no. This can't be. There's got to be a mistake."

"I'm afraid it's not a mistake, but there is another test for me tomorrow. You are scheduled to take this group to India tomorrow too, and I want you to go ahead with it. It's okay. That is important work and I don't want to stop you from it."

"Chuck, I can't hear all this and just leave. This is a time to stick together, to fight this thing side by side. I can't do that."

"Yes, I know but those people on your team haven't traveled outside the United States before, and you know how difficult a trip to India can be. There are always problems somewhere."

What a night trying to face all of this. We considered the cancer. Was it really cancer? The timing. How can we change the trip or change the tests? We can't. The trip. It was for two weeks. Could we postpone it? Or cancel it? Could someone else lead the trip? No one else would have a visa to enter the country. You can't get a substitute with a visa that quick. What a night. What agony.

We finally decided that I would go ahead and take the group to India. Going into India is such a challenge and most of these people had never been out of the United States and didn't have a clue how to jump through the hoops of international travel. After I delivered them to Samuel Stephens, I would catch the next plane home. This would take three days to get there and back. It looked like days were precious but three days were a lot better than the two weeks that the trip was scheduled.

Those days that I was gone gave Chuck an opportunity to make his plans. He made a list of all the things he wanted to do before he died. His list included things like changing the car titles, replacing the driveway, getting the house painted, and everything he could think of to help me when he was gone. Chuck also decided to write a letter to his five grandchildren on each of their birthdays until they were sixteen. He did that for his grandson Bryson, who was five years old. He started on letters to Erin, our ten-year-old granddaughter, but wasn't able to finish.

After I returned from India, my total attention was in taking care of my husband. He took me to the local hospice office. (Shall I say he dragged me?) I didn't want to go. It was too hard to conceive that we were going to need their services. I was denying the finality of this disease.

We decided we wanted a second opinion. Perhaps the hospital in Cincinnati was wrong and there was something that could be done. Our son Mark (now also called Chuck by his wife and friends) made arrangements at Mayo Clinic in Rochester, Minnesota, and we flew up there. But the report was the same. They confirmed the cancer, telling Chuck he would be fortunate to live three months.

At home Chuck set to work on his lists. First we went to our attorney to see if his will was in order. That was hard. There we were talking about him not being here anymore. The hardest part was taking his name off the car titles and putting mine on. That seemed so final. And it was. But this was only the beginning.

In only three weeks I knew this was it. He was getting weaker and was starting to throw up—we needed the help of hospice. They would be there for us. I called them on a Sunday and even though it was not a workday, one of their staff came out to the house to get things started. They provided the medicine he needed and told me how to administer it. They sent a nurse to the house twice a week or when necessary. Because I needed to be at the office some during the day, they provided people to come stay with Chuck so he wasn't by himself. Over all, they enabled me to keep him at home those remaining precious days.

The Project Partner staff was left to work a great deal on their own during this time. Yes, I did go in for about an hour a day, but my attention was on taking care of Chuck. I sensed that there was trouble brewing there, but I dismissed it, thinking I could deal with it later. Once, I spent a long session on the phone on some of the problems while we were at the Mayo Clinic. Even when a staff member came to me and said he would take the job of president, I dismissed the issue for a later time.

In February, we brought all the family in for a last reunion. In the last weeks, others came as well. Visitors came from many cities across the United States and even from India, Nicaragua, Haiti, and Mexico. Eighty-seven days after Chuck's cancer was first diagnosed, he was gone.

This was all inconceivable to me. We were married forty-five years, always did everything together working as a team, and now he was gone. I was in a daze. Where was my purpose in living now? How would I stumble through each day? I was surely walking in a thick darkness. Surely, surely this was just all a bad dream.

Never Will I Leave You, Never Will I Forsake You

A few days after the burial, when I was able to get back to the office, I discovered the extent of the troubles I assumed were minor were not. The staff leaders formed their own plans, and they didn't include me. Although I worked with Chuck to start the organization and was president for eight years, hired everyone who worked there, and recruited all the board members, things were different now. I struggled to hold my ground, but it wasn't long before the leaders who emerged convinced the board that I now was not only incapable, but had never functioned adequately, although in those eight years, the Lord had enabled me to more than double the ministry and the income. I just couldn't believe it, but there was a plan to take the organization away from me.

In order to get away and collect my thoughts, and to pray for help in this darkness, I chose to go visit a friend in Colorado. Maybe I could find an answer if I was away from the conflict for a bit.

We had special friends in the Glenwood Springs area because that was our vacation ground all those years we lived in Wichita. We used to take our boys, load up the camper, and be gone for two weeks. During those times we became acquainted with a group who had trail bikes called Tote Gotes. We loved those times and we enjoyed those Tote Gotes, even ended up getting two of them for our family.

The group knew that Chuck was a preacher, so they would have him lead them in songs, prayer, and special mountainside church services. We were able to minister to them. They looked to him as their pastor. During those times we went with them over many of Colorado's back roads and mountain passes.

Going out to Glenwood on I-70 we always drove over Loveland Pass. This pass is nearly twelve thousand feet high, with spectacular scenery. The mountains were always so beautiful and majestic to us, and we surely enjoyed every part of that mountain road. By this trip, the state of Colorado had put in the Eisenhower Tunnel to make it easier on motorists and replacing the need to go over the pass.

I had a wonderful visit, as expected, but it was time to return and face the issues. I left Glenwood that beautiful summer day heading east on I-70. Every mile of the way there was something to remember about Chuck and our times together. There was the Glenwood Canyon and the places we stopped for lunch. Further on was the road we always turned on to go up to the Flattops. That was a special place to us as it was so remote and we liked that. We even had a special camping spot. Up there we could have the mountains to ourselves, or so we thought.

Then came the turn off to Eagle where we usually headed south to a special campground. On down the road was Aspen. Oh yes, memories of lunches there and once going horseback riding on a ranch nearby. Next came Dillon, which was really growing these days, and changing a lot from the earlier times.

Ahead of me was a choice: the Eisenhower Tunnel or Loveland Pass. I decided to take the Pass because of all the memories. This was easy. No traffic, as all the cars and trucks were using the Tunnel. I enjoyed the climb as the road rose ahead with each hairpin turn and switchback. There used to be many cars at the top. People would come here and go up even higher on some of the trails. But that day there wasn't a soul around. The area was deserted.

Stopping my car, I got out to look again at the majestic mountains. How I always enjoyed them. This time, however, it was lonesome, so lonesome. Chuck wasn't with me. He never would be with me again. It was so lonely without him. I needed him, and I needed him to help me with this big problem at the office. I was suddenly consumed with grief and so shaken with emotion that I lost my balance and fell. Lying there on the ground a surprising thought came into my mind: "You can go be with Chuck. You don't have to be lonely. This could be really easy. See these roads and these curves. See these cliffs. You can easily drive your car over one of those cliffs and you won't have to worry about anything around here again. You won't have to worry about the office, or what is happening. You won't have to worry about finances, or ... anything. You can be with Chuck."

I turned around to see if anyone else was there, but there was no one. I jumped up and ran to the car. I needed to leave there. I had to talk to someone, to get away from this. Never in my life did I think of suicide and there it was surrounding me, pushing me down. I had to get away ... and fast. Putting the car in gear, I hurried down the mountain toward Denver as fast as possible, praying all the way. I wanted to call my friend and pastor, Claude Robold, and tell him what happened. I wanted to talk to someone, someone who cared.

I did get down to Denver and I did call Claude, but he wasn't in. By then it didn't matter. I was back to level thinking. The Lord heard my prayer. The temptation was over, and Christ gave his victory. I needed his strength for what was to come next.

A Thick Darkness

I knew the Lord was with me on the mountain, but the problems at the office were still there when I returned to Ohio. Conflict arose on a daily basis. The spirit at the office was one of hostility and anger, and the behavior wasn't what one expected in a Christian organization. There was even a day when two vice presidents came in my office and yelled at me because they didn't like my decision. This behavior was totally foreign to me. I tried to tell the board members what was happening, but they were getting other stories. There were unbelievable situations. Within five months I could see that I had lost the battle. The board members had come to believe that I was incompetent.

These vice presidents were capable men. They came into Project Partner because they believed in its ministry. They wanted to move on, and they had plans to do so. They had their purposes in mind for the ministry and they didn't want me around. I was a woman and a widow. They wanted the control. They wanted my name to stay with the organization, but they did not want any of my input or direction.

It took a phone call from my son to bring me out of the fog. He said, "Mom, what has happened to you? This isn't like you. What do you want, and what do you think dad would want?"

This brought me to my knees before God again. What were my non-negotiables? What could I allow and when couldn't I compromise? I called it my "line in the sand" moment. I realized I gave in and almost gave up, but that wasn't what I was supposed to do.

I had two options—to fight or to resign. It was still only six months since Chuck had died. I didn't have it in me to fight. I hurt so bad. This hurt so bad. *Why won't they listen to me? This is Chuck's and my ministry.* We had started it together, prayed over it, put our own money in it, and worked at it for over twenty-five years. *What could I do now?* I could not fight. Resigning was something I never considered until then. It seemed like another death. Project Partner had been our life's purpose and joy for twenty-five years. This ministry was what God called us to do. Where was Chuck when I needed him? And God, where was he?

The day came that I took my desk, my papers, my books, and all of my possessions from the office. My son, Paul, came and helped me move everything home. I was finished there. I was not wanted any more. I felt I had been crucified. That is, I felt I had been torn from my life without cause. It hurt so badly. That was my life. All the relationships there were Chuck's and mine. The nationals were my friends. The contributors believed in me. Then what about the assets? *How do I respond? And where do I go from here?*

I had three trusted friends with whom I felt I could share this situation. With their help, the Lord led me through this difficult period of my life. I knew in my head that I needed to forgive these leaders but my heart had problems with that. I was in the depth of depression and the depth of despair, but somehow I also knew that the Lord wasn't finished with me yet.

There is an important principle in Christian discipleship that seems to be hidden. One that is seldom talked about or even recognized. We seem to pretend that it never happens and is not a part of the Christian walk. It took going through this experience for me to see that it happens regularly and that it isn't to be shunned. It can produce tremendous growth and benefit if we let it. It is being crucified in your ministry.

I learned that when it happens, you can't fight back. You can't be angry. And you can't broadcast your problems. You can't even hold a grudge. You have to forgive. You have to forget. And you have to love them. You have to turn it over to the Lord. You have to move on.

Two books helped me work through this time and choose the Lord's response. *The Tale of Two Kings* and *Crucified by Christians* are both written by Gene Edwards. Edwards beautifully shows that God chose his only son for crucifixion. God chooses who will be crucified. It is an honor to be chosen.

Researching the response of Jesus, I discovered no malice or hatred in his heart. No, he didn't want to go through it, but he went through it with the spirit of forgiveness. And afterward, did he broadcast to the world what those terrible Pharisees did to him? Never. He didn't mention it. He chose to move on with his ministry and fulfill the mission that his Father gave him.

It takes the mighty grace of God to follow the footsteps of our Savior through a crucifixion experience. God gave me himself and those three friends who led me through it with their prayers, their correction at times, and their belief in me. Looking back, I can now see the hand of the Lord. It was right. It was God's plan. And God was taking care of me.

Chuck's death helped me see that our purpose in life is not to achieve wealth and fame but to please God. We are not here long, but during our time, our generation, we are to allow God to use us as he wishes for his purposes. I discovered Acts 13:36, and placed that scripture on Chuck's grave, finding it most appropriate: "For when David had served God's purpose in his own generation, he fell asleep."

The other death, the crucifixion, taught me even more. Who wants to go through a crucifixion? No one. But when you do, the Lord goes with you. Many good things have happened that never would have if I hadn't lived that experience. The Lord does know what he is doing and what is ahead for us. We are to please God, make our actions and reactions like his, and he will lead us, bless us, and enable us to fulfill the plans God has for us. Now what could be greater?

CHAPTER 11

MIRACLES: CHOOSE YOUR RESPONSE

D o you believe in miracles? Let me tell you about one that I think is comparable to the parting of the Red Sea. Who ever heard that after a hostile takeover, a corporation was returned to its founder?

While still reeling from the board meeting when I lost Project Partner, I went to Mexico to see Enrique Cepeda. He had worked with me for twenty-eight years, he knew my heart, he knew my present distress, and I needed someone to talk with.

The visit was just what I needed; so was what happened next. The day before I was to leave and return home, I was with Enrique and his brother, Eleazar. Eleazar was a pastor, just started a new church, and wanted me to see his facilities. An office building was being remodeled, and as I was walking around ladders and smiling at workers, my thoughts were dwelling on my loss. Suddenly Eleazar said, "Donna, I have been praying for you and I have a message for you from the Lord."

"What do you mean you have a message for me?" I replied.

"Donna," he continued, " the message is in Revelation 3:8. It says 'See, I have placed before you an open door that no one can shut, I know that you have little strength, yet you have kept my word and have not denied my name.' "

"Thanks, Eleazar. I appreciate your help." That was my outward response, but inwardly I was thinking, *What is he talking about?* I soon forgot his message, even though I did write it down in my prayer journal for that day, January 17, 1993.

Confused as I was at this time, I was wondering if I still had ministry to do. Was the Lord finished with me, or did he still have plans for me? I thought about starting another organization, but it would send a message of Christian conflict and I didn't want that. As the days and months moved by, there came a time that I did as Abraham did. I call it "going to Mount Moriah." Like Abraham, the Lord called me to make a sacrifice. I was to sacrifice my ministry as I knew it.

Samuel Stephens was urging me to come over to India for a couple of weeks and just be with him and his wife, Prati. While there they could pray with me and I could see if I should still be involved in this kind of work. I decided to go. The trip over to India was lonely, but when I got there, I was where I belonged. Yes, I still had this kind of ministry on my heart. "The Lord isn't finished with me yet," was the message that I heard.

It wasn't long after I went to my Mount Moriah that two of the national leaders I worked with contacted me. They ended their relationship with Project Partner because of internal situations that were creating problems for them. They were ready to talk about beginning again with me.

Looking back now, I can see several steps that the Lord was taking in this restoration process. I am convinced that if I decided to fight, the Lord would not have worked his miracle for me. Because I let it go with my Mount Moriah decision, I was totally unaware of all that was going on. I had no contact with anyone who knew what was happening.

God's Intervention

Next came the miracle. The board members were challenged by a previous member of the board of directors who came uninvited to the annual meeting in October 1993. The board of Project Partner offered the ministry back to me. God spoke to their hearts. Specifically, they offered to return the ministry I developed with the foreign national leaders. At that time, the assets of the corporation were worth nearly one million dollars.

Both Samuel Stephens and Enrique Cepeda were at my house at the time. They were to get Ohio driver's licenses that day. Then the phone rang. The board of directors was in session, and they asked me to come over to the office for the purpose of returning Project Partner to me. I couldn't believe my ears. Laying the phone down, I consulted with both Samuel and Enrique as to what to do. They encouraged me to go and even offered to go with me.

I listened intently as the board chairperson explained their offer. Yes, I accepted it. They told me I could have the ministry and assets effective January 1, 1994. That was more than two months away. An immediate concern raced through my mind as to what would happen during those two months. Then the Lord gave me his assurance that if he could restore Project Partner to me, he could take care of it for those two months. I chose to start over with no board and no staff, replacing them as I could. I announced my decision on the spot.

The next day as I was driving home, my mind replayed all that happened. The Lord certainly produced a miracle. Truthfully, I did not really expected God's intervention in such a marvelous way. I had not listened to Eleazar's message. I did not really trust the Lord to this extent. It was at this point that a message came to my spirit from the Lord. "My child, why do you doubt? I will take care of you. I have my plans for you." It was so strong that I stopped my car, grabbed a pencil and paper, and wrote it down. That was precious. "My child," a term of endearment. "Why do you doubt?" a gentle rebuke. "I will take care of you. I have my plans for you," a declaration of his tender care. Oh, what a Heavenly Father we have!

It wasn't until March 1994, five months later, that I remembered what Enrique's brother, Eleazar, had told me. I was in Egypt with one of our teams holding a pastors' training conference. One particular session was all in Arabic, so I was just sitting in the back of the room reading my Bible. I came to Revelation 3:8. "See, I have placed before you an open door that no one can shut. I know that you have little strength, yet you have kept my word and have not denied my name." I realized then that was what Eleazar told me right at the beginning of my loss and I forgot all about it. The Lord sent a messenger to encourage me and I did not recognize it. But there it was. He was taking care of me all the time.

Seeing Problems As Opportunities

Years before we had a monumental problem which the Lord used for his glory. Our forty-passenger airplane took off from the Akron-Canton, Ohio, airport in 1974. This was going to be one of our best workcamps. The team included people from Canada, Michigan, and Ohio who responded to the opportunity to go on a work camp in the Caribbean. This workcamp team was unique, as it was to build a school in Haiti and a parsonage in Jamaica and would get Christians from four countries—Canada, the United States, Jamaica, and Haiti—working together.

The plane landed in Kingston, Jamaica, to drop off about half of our team to work on that island with the Jamaicans. A group of Jamaicans boarded the plane and flew on with the rest of the team to Haiti to work together there. We had two work-camps going at the same time with Christians from these four countries side by side.

The most direct way was to fly over Cuba, and we had the Cuban government's permission to do so. We did it several times before on our trips to Haiti or Jamaica. There were two air corridors open, and we filed for permission, giving the Cuban officials the necessary forms and the passenger list. With our permit, we flew the team from Fort Lauderdale, Florida, across Cuba without a concern.

The Haiti workcamp went well. The school building was completed. The crew loaded the plane and flew the team back to Kingston, Jamaica. Claude Ferguson, the team leader, led the group in a farewell circle with the team before they boarded the plane for the final legs of the flight back to Fort Lauderdale and the Akron-Canton airport.

Our pilots, Don Shaver and Dick Sanders, made the necessary flight arrangements, called in their flight plan, and were soon on their way toward home. On entering Cuban airspace

Claude was in the cockpit explaining the instrumentation to Terry McLaughlin, one of the workcampers. He saw a jet on the western horizon. Incredulous, he said to Dick and Don, "Is that a Bandit?" in reference to an old war movie. It turned out that it really was. Then that MiG-21 and another one just like it came close to our airplane and shook it with his jet blast.

"Wow," Dick exclaimed, "He sure made a mistake in coming that close to us." He immediately called Cuban air traffic control, who said they didn't know what the MiGs were doing up there. In a few minutes air traffic control called back, "Convair 90844, ascend to 27,000 feet."

Immediately three MiG-17s appeared, and one of them pulled right alongside Dick Sanders' window on the right of our plane and dropped his landing gear. "That's a military signal to land," Dick called out.

At that moment a message was received from the Cuban air traffic controller. His voice barked, "Convair 90844, proceed to the airport at Camaguay and land there."

Dick picked up his microphone and responded, "Cuba Air Traffic Control, this is Convair 90844. We had prior permission to fly direct to Fort Lauderdale, Florida."

"Convair 90844, you are to land immediately at Camaguay," was their harsh response. At that point the three MiG-17 Russian airplanes started circling the Convair. The wake of their turbulence created a lot of bouncing around as well as immediate fear and panic.

Claude Ferguson, the team leader had sent the workcamper back to his seat and then returned to the cockpit to find out what was going on. Don, the captain, was visibly shaking as he turned the plane in the direction of Camaguay. Dick briefly told Claude what was going on, but they knew that they were in trouble. Claude, feeling the intense fear that was filling the cabin of the plane, picked up the intercom mike and started praying. They needed the help of the Lord and they needed him now. They were totally at the mercy of the Cuban government. As Claude closed his prayer and said, "Amen," there was suddenly a soft calmness that came over everyone on board. They could feel the peace of the Lord. It gave them time to take pictures of those MiGs and wait with expectancy to see how the Lord was going to take care of them.

The plane landed in Camaguay as directed. As it taxied over to the terminal, those on board saw that one of the MiGs landing behind them had actually run off the end of the runway. The terminal was poorly lit with only two distant lights, but they could see there were officials waiting for them. Turning off the right engine, they let down the stairs to allow the Cuban officials to come on board. Claude met them at the top of the stairs. "Get everyone off this plane and inside now. They are not to take anything with them" commanded the official with the most military badges in his best English.

The team quickly started disembarking as he ordered. Yet, in spite of the darkness, the fact that they had been forced to land in Cuba, and now being told to get off the plane, there was still that sense of peace that the Lord gave them as they prayed. They were escorted into a rather small room with chairs in a circle. As they each took a seat, they realized that there were exactly thirty-eight chairs, one for each of them from the plane. Claude quickly remembered that the Cubans had the passenger manifest. They knew there were thirty-eight people on the plane plus the crew. They had their names and hometowns. Why were they forced to land with permission to overfly Cuba? He turned to talk with Don and Dick only to find that they, along with Bobbie Feiring, the stewardess, had been taken to another room, presumably for interrogation.

What Claude didn't know was that Castro was entertaining East German communists at that time. Castro was going to show his guests what he could do with an American airplane. The official counted the people, checked off their names from the list, and had the five Canadians sit together. They were told that they would be released to go on home to Canada. Cuba had diplomatic relations with Canada and even airline service to Toronto. They were then told that all the Americans were not going to be released. The Canadians emphatically stated that they would not leave without their American friends. They were in this together, they said.

The group still had that peace and assurance from the Lord. Worry was not on their agenda. They were treated well, and although they were not free to go and were certainly being detained, they were finding it an adventure. Since they were in Cuba and since they knew a few Christian songs in Spanish, they raised the windows of their dining room and sang those songs at the top of their voices, even ending with "God Bless America"— a bold stand in this Communist country in 1974. Meanwhile back in Wichita, I received a phone call from the US State Department. "Are you aware that your plane is down in Cuba?"

My mental response was, *I don't know what you are talking about. What are you saying?* We always monitored the plane on these workcamp trips. The team leader would call when they were getting ready to leave the airport heading for their next destination, giving us the approximate time of arrival there. When they got there, they always called so we knew where they were. Since they called from Kingston, I was expecting a call from them on their arrival at Fort Lauderdale. So how did the State Department get in this?

"What do we do?" I finally blurted out. The State Department official said we were to stay by the phone and they would be in touch with us. We had a sizable staff, but besides the ones on the plane, the rest were all out of town that week-end. Only Chuck and I were monitoring this group and the plane's flight.

We had a pastor friend in Washington, DC, the Reverend Sam Hines, who knew about our plane. One of his parishioners worked at the State Department and was the first to know of our problem, even before we did. He contacted Pastor Hines, who realized the severity of the situation and pulled together a prayer team immediately.

It wasn't long before the phone rang again. This time the State Department official was saying that Cuba was demanding

$3,000 in cash to be sent to them immediately through the Swiss Embassy.

This was Saturday afternoon. We certainly didn't have any cash and especially not that amount. That was a lot of money in 1974. Chuck picked up the Wichita phone book, hurriedly looking for the name of the President of Boulevard State Bank, Robert McGrath, where we had our account. As he dialed his number, Chuck was also praying for the Lord to help him find the answers. After Chuck explained the situation, McGrath told Chuck that there was a bank open on Saturday afternoon at the Twin Lakes Shopping Center. He would call them and tell them to cash a $3,000 check for us.

Chuck hurried to get this done and wired the funds to the Swiss Embassy as quickly as possible, then we waited for the next phone call from the State Department. When it did come, we weren't prepared. The Cubans wanted more money. This time it was $5,000 in cash, and by now the bank at Twin Lakes was closed. The State Department official added, "You need to comply as quickly as possible to meet their demands. Send the $5,000 by Western Union as soon as possible."

"Sir," I responded, "We've never had anything like this happen before. What is it going to take to get our people out of Cuba? How can we get Castro to release them? How much money is he going to demand? How long will he keep them? Are they okay? Are they in any danger?"

"In any hostage situation similar to this, it has usually been two to three weeks," said the official. "Once it was only five days. You would be very lucky if it were only five days, and there is no way of knowing how much money they will demand. All we can do at this point is to meet their demands as quickly as possible. The Swiss Embassy will help us stay in contact with them and also be our advocate. We will call you immediately when we have any more word from Cuba."

Chuck put in a call to our bank president again. "Bob, Cuba is demanding more money. Now they want $5,000 in cash. What can we do? We don't have that kind of money in our account."

"That's okay, Chuck," he replied, "I'll send Gary (one of his vice presidents) to our bank, and he can open it up and get you the money.

"What shall I do about all this money we are getting? Shall I sign some kind of note?" Chuck asked.

"That's okay. Just come in Monday and take care of it. No, you had better make it Tuesday because you've got lots to do to take care of all of this," he graciously responded.

Arriving at the bank, Chuck was met by the vice president, the police, and two men from the electric company. It was going to take some major work to get money out of the bank at that time on Saturday night. But they did it. The vice president decided a cashier's check would work and pecked out one on the typewriter for $5,000.

"Chuck," Gary injected, "you just might need some more money before the evening is over." He was pecking out another cashier's check for $2,000. "Just come in Tuesday and we'll see what we can work out."

About this time I called a reporter friend at the Wichita Eagle newspaper telling him I thought I had a story for him, but I didn't want to tell him what it was yet. In a few minutes he was knocking on the office door.

"Mike, I really have a story for you and it's one you can send out across the United States. Remember our airplane? You went with us on that workcamp to Managua after the earthquake there. Well, this is a bigger story. Castro has forced our team to land in Camaguay. There are thirty-eight people on board from Ohio and Canada plus our crew. They have already demanded $8,000 from us and we don't know what else they are going to want. The State Department is our go-between, along with the Swiss Embassy, so we are just waiting it out until they tell us what they want next."

Mike was busy writing down everything we could tell him, and then he gathered up his notes to hurry back to the newspaper. Heading for the door, he quickly turned, reached in his billfold, and pulled out some money. "Here's a start on all the money that you are going to need. I'll stay in touch."

It was now dark and time for the plane to arrive at the Akron-Canton airport. The time came when we had to let the families of the people on board know what happened. Chuck called our pastor friend in Canton, Marvin Cain, and told him the news. He volunteered to get all the families of the team together and help them through this crisis.

It only took about fifteen minutes for the news to break across the United States. The first call was from a radio station in Canton. Then came calls from Miami, the *New York Times,* the *Los Angeles Times,* and others as they found out. Numerous calls throughout the night from ABC, CBS, and NBC put us on first name basis with their reporters.

Early Sunday morning Chuck asked me to cover for him at church. The phones were ringing constantly, and he continued to be available. We were in touch with the State Department at least every hour, although they didn't have any answers for us. Radio stations, TV stations, and newspapers were calling for more information.

That morning the front page of newspapers around the world told of the missionary airplane that was down in Cuba. We later discovered it was the lead story in Europe, Egypt, Peru, Haiti, Mexico, the Philippines, and even in the *Stars and Stripes,* our United States military paper in the Indian Ocean. There it was for all to see. Now churches started to call to see if it really was Project Partner and what they could do. People who had been on workcamps with us knew it was our plane and started praying. Chuck's response to all was "Pray!" And pray they must have. I know we did at our church. At 1:30 that afternoon Chuck received a call from the State Department telling him that the plane and all the passengers were released and on their way to Fort Lauderdale. Castro let them go, and did not asked for any more money.

In the end, they all came home with a great adventure story. No one was hurt. They were released in twenty-five hours. It had cost us $8,000 plus some extra expenses. The Lord indeed produced a miracle. But he wasn't finished yet.

The next week we sent out a letter to the friends and donors of Project Partner asking for help. They responded by more than covering the amount we gave to Castro, sending in more than $12,000. Wanting the funds to be used for Cuba, Chuck discovered an evangelist friend in Canada who was going to Cuba in a few months. He agreed to take the remaining funds and give them to some of the Cuban churches to help them in their work.

There were several miracles here. The Lord delivered and protected his people. He provided the resources. He gave us millions of dollars in publicity all around the world. We went through a trauma and there was no damage. The Lord provided.

All those wonderful miracles in the Bible started with a problem. One thing I have discovered is if you don't have a problem, you don't need a miracle.

CHAPTER 12

MOUNTAINS: A MOUNTAIN IN CHINA

That first trip to China in 1981 included the adventure of meeting Wang and dealing with his question about how our religion helps us with our problems. But there was another adventure in that trip. I call it my "James Bond" adventure.

Before we left Hong Kong to go to Beijing and Shanghai, a friend took us to visit Dr. Jonathan Chao, the president of the Chinese Research Center. He took the time to tell us what was going on in China. Researchers were beginning to get information from China and find out how the church had survived those years of persecution and terror. In 1950, Mao Tse-tung, the Communist dictator, took over China and forced all missionaries to leave. The Bamboo Curtain went down, shutting out any news for some thirty-plus years.

When the missionaries left, there were fewer than 1 million Christians. We in the West didn't know if the church died or if any Christians remained. We had heard that the Cultural Revolution was bad, whatever that meant. News was coming out of China, and Jonathan and his workers were monitoring the radio broadcasts, newspapers, letters, and anything else they could get. The borders were still closed and getting in and out of China was very difficult, we were told.

We were going in. To do that we had to get a special visa. We would be under the complete authority of the China Travel Agency all the time we were there and the agency would dictate our schedule and plans for us. They would monitor everything we did.

Jonathan informed me of the great need for Bibles in China. Then he asked me if I would take some with me. My immediate thought was *I didn't bargain for this. I'm not sure I can do it.*

Jonathan continued, "There won't be any problem for you. It is not really illegal. If the authorities would find the Bibles, they would simply take them away and return them to you when you leave to come back to Hong Kong. There shouldn't be any problem at all," he said.

"Okay, if it's no big deal, I'll try it. How many are you talking about?" I asked.

"I have one hundred here ready for you to take. They are small and black with no printing on the outside, so they won't be recognized," he replied.

Well, I didn't recognize them as Bibles and since they were in Chinese, I couldn't figure out if I was holding them right side up or upside down. "Here is the man's name to give them to," Jonathan explained. "It's Mr. Pei. And on this other piece of paper is his phone number. You might want to put them in different places in your purse in case someone goes through your purse." He spoke rather softly as he said that last comment.

I hadn't bargained for that, but by this point I felt that I was already committed and didn't want to back out. *"After all, they are Bibles and I do want the Chinese to have Bibles, don't I?" I asked myself.*

"Don't use the word Bible," he continued. "Instead use the word gifts. Your room will probably be bugged."

This was getting more complicated all the time. Maybe Jonathan thought I was the kind of person who would like to do this sort of thing.

He told me when I get to Shanghai to call Mr. Pei and he would meet me and take the Bibles. I asked him if this was all there was to it, and he assured me. "Yes, it will be simple." That was all the instruction I received.

According to Jonathan, Bibles were rare in China because in the '60s they were all confiscated and burned. They closed the churches and used the buildings for storage or turned them into Communist headquarters. Most pastors were put in prison. Chinese Christians were very anxious to get Bibles.

Having done nothing like this before, we took the Bibles to our hotel room, put them in the middle of the floor, and prayed over them. "Lord, let us get these Bibles into China." Then we wrapped them with our clothes, hid them in our suitcases as well as we knew how, and headed for the airport.

At the Hong Kong airport the China government added eight people to our tour group. Since I spoke English, the China Travel Agency simply assigned all English-speaking people to me. Two girls were from Australia, where they worked for Quantas Airlines. Peter was from Denmark and was working for British Airways. One man was from New Zealand, two missionaries were from Japan, and two young men were from Detroit. The latter two were going around the world, and this was near the end of their trip.

Our first stop was Beijing, and I was nervous. We went through immigration easily and headed on to pick up our bags and go through customs. We waited and waited for those bags. The conveyor belt just kept going round and round with nothing on it. The more I watched it, the more anxious I became. I was sitting there chewing my fingernails. *"Are they going to find the Bibles? Will I get in trouble? Okay Lord, help me do this, please help me. I can't imagine what they will do to me if they catch me with these Bibles. What have I gotten myself into?"*

For an hour we waited, and finally the bags appeared on the conveyer. I had plenty of time to pray and chew my fingernails. We grabbed them and headed for customs. When we got there the official asked me if we were a group. When I told them we were, they just motioned for us to go on through. No problem at all. Just like Jonathan said.

We spent those few days in Beijing with Wang as our guide, and then we flew on to Shanghai on Sunday afternoon. The hotel there was a little better than Beijing, but not much. The front doors to all hotels were sealed shut in those days so no one could use them. We had to use the side entrance. No Chinese were allowed in the hotel except staff. The hotel was only for foreigners, and they wanted to keep us separate. It was a long drive to the side entrance and a big fence around everything.

I went to the desk and got the keys for all our rooms and passed them among our group. Now I was to go to my room and make that call to Mr. Pei, but first I had to figure out how to use the telephone in China. Telephones look basically the same in every country but the telephone system is always different. How was I to do this? I sure can't ask for help. That would be a good way to get in trouble. I experimented a bit and managed to get a phone line out of the hotel. I dialed the number, the phone rang, and a woman answered in Chinese. Somehow I didn't expect this. Doing something like this was so totally new to me.

"Is Mr. Pei there?" I stammered. She said something I could not understand and then the phone was silent. I didn't know if she said, "Lady, you have the wrong number," or if she had left the phone to get him.

After what seemed an extensive wait, Mr. Pei answered in English. What a relief! "Mr. Pei," I said, "I am Donna Thomas from America. I have a small group here with me. We were just in Hong Kong and met some great people there. They asked me to give you their greetings. Also, we have brought some gifts for you."

"Oh, fine," he replied.

"Where can I meet you and give you these gifts?"

"What is your schedule for tomorrow?" he asked.

"Well, we'll be going to a Commune (a community of people assigned to live and work together for the government) in the morning and then the guide said we'd be at a botanical garden in the afternoon. Oh yes, we will be at the Number One Department Store tomorrow at 5:00 P.M. Would that work out all right?"

"That will be fine. Where should I meet you?" he responded.

That caught me off guard. I hadn't figured this all out yet. *Let's see, what would be in a department store in China?* I thought. *Every department store I have ever been in has a shoe*

*department. Surely they have one in China department store
too. Yes, that would probably be a good place to meet."* "How
about in the shoe department?"

"That will be fine," he replied. Then another question.
"How will I know you?"

I thought he *could* probably tell who I was since I look like
an American, but I didn't say that. "Well, I'll have on a yellow
blouse and a blue skirt," was my answer.

The next morning as we met for breakfast, I discovered we
had a different guide who was very pro-government. He had
been taught to think "the end justifies the means." Whatever it
took to have Communism for the whole world was worth it even
if it meant killing people. I knew I didn't have a friend here, and
that he surely didn't need to know what we were doing.

I got the group with the Bibles on the bus early. It was
October, so they could use their coats to cover their packages. I
suggested that they sit in the back of the bus and let the eight
new people sit in the front so hopefully the guide would not
know what was going on. *What would I do if he found out?* I
thought to myself.

Our first stop was the Commune. There were eighteen
thousand people living in this place, all under government
control. They all worked for a common cause. It didn't matter
if a person was lazy or worked hard. All got the same pay. As
you could guess, there weren't very many hard workers.

We went first to the headquarters where the leaders there sat
us down around a table for tea. They brought each one a typical
Chinese cup with lid filled with sweet smelling Jasmine tea. As
we sipped the tea, they shared the glories of Communism and
how great it was living in a Commune. Then they took us to a
kindergarten. The children were waiting for us and presented
a special program. Next was their hospital, which in my
estimation left a hundred thousand things to be desired. But we
did see acupuncture being practiced, and that was certainly
different. Then, before lunch, we stopped at a factory and made
a tour of their premises. There were lots of workers, but there

weren't any working very hard. The whole factory seemed in slow motion.

Lunch was unbelievable. We were served twenty-seven courses. After ten courses I stopped eating. When I asked what happened to the leftovers, I was told that there was plenty of food and leftovers were simply thrown away. I didn't believe that because our guide had already shown us some of their homes. He took us through a display house, with a small but adequate living space, a small bedroom, and a wee little kitchen in the back. The bed had a board for the mattress, and the kitchen had a wood burning stove and a bucket to carry in water. There was a television in their "typical" house; however, there were no electric outlets in any of the rooms or any electric lights. Obviously the television was there just for show. We were supposed to appreciate the great accommodations that the government provided for the people. This was the People's Republic of China, after all.

We then got back on the bus and our guide told us that he had good news for us. He had been able to rearrange our schedule, and he was excited about that. We were going to get to see the Children's Palace that afternoon. They had planned a special program for us. Therefore, he would speed up all the previously scheduled afternoon activities.

I hadn't planned for something like this. I questioned him on how the schedule was going to be changed and at what time we were going to be at the department store. He said we would be moving everything up so we would be at the department store at 3:00 P.M. now instead of 5:00 P.M. *Oh my, I thought. We will be there and gone before Mr. Pei will come. My heart sank. How do I handle this? How is the Lord going to make our appointment work?*

The next stop was the Botanical Gardens. We filed off the bus and followed our guide down the path between the plants. I didn't go far because I was asking the Lord, "What am I supposed to do now? There's no phone here to call him. I don't know how to handle this."

Turning around, I went back to the bus, climbed on board, and sat down halfway back. I needed to pray and think. Then I noticed that the bus driver was studying a little book of English. Maybe he could help me. Going up to him I held my right hand to my mouth and ear like a telephone saying "Hello, hello."

He knew what I wanted. Jumping out of his driver's seat, he motioned for me to follow him. We went down a different path, back through some trees to a little cabin. Inside there was a telephone. Great! Now to figure out how to use this one.

I got it to work the first time, it rang, and the same lady answered in Chinese. When I asked again for Mr. Pei, the phone went silent. I felt more comfortable waiting this time, and shortly he answered. I told him of the schedule changes. He told me that it was no problem and that he would be there at the new time. Wow! Thank you, Lord. This delivering Bibles was getting to be a bit more than I bargained for. It was supposed to be simple.

When we all got back on the bus, I told my group of the change in plans but that it was going to work out. They were to follow me in the store and I would give him the Bibles I had first. Then they would come up one at a time and give him the Bibles they had.

At the Number One Department Store I asked Peter, who knew what the plan was, if he would keep the guide occupied. I sure didn't want that guide to know what we were doing. He suggested that he would take the guide to the electronic department.

As we entered the store the guide began to tell us about the store and where each department was located. That was better than I could have dreamed. He actually told us that the shoe department was on the second floor. That made me feel more comfortable. Then he took us all to the fourth floor to start our excursion, and that was where the electronics were located. This was getting better.

Peter took the guide over to the radios to ask him questions, and the rest of us headed quickly for the stairs to go down to the second floor and the shoe department.

Finding a pillar to stand by, I stopped there, looking very American in my yellow blouse and blue skirt. Soon this nice looking older Chinese man came over and introduced himself as Mr. Pei. He seemed a bit nervous, so I gave him the Bibles I had. Then one of the group came up and handed him his sack, then another, and then I realized we had a new problem. Obviously I had never done anything like this before and didn't have everything figured out. The amount of Bibles that eight people had brought in could not be carried out by one person. Too big a load. I hadn't thought of that.

"Mr. Pei, how can we get the rest of these gifts to you?"

"Where are you staying?" he asked.

I really didn't know where we were staying. I pulled out the room key with the tag on it, but it was in Chinese. It didn't mean anything to me. He looked at it, though, and recognized the hotel.

"Call me when you get back and I will meet you nearby," was his reply. He took the Bibles he had with him and quickly disappeared.

Our tour continued with the program at the Children's Palace, then dinner, and afterwards to a Chinese ballet. The guide added these activities especially for us, so I told him that he, being so kind to us, didn't have to take us back to the hotel. We could make it fine by ourselves and the bus driver. He thought that was a great idea and told us he'd see us in the morning. Great. We were by ourselves. That was a relief.

Back at the hotel I headed for the phone again and called Mr. Pei. He directed me to meet him out on the street, a bit further up than the hotel, with the "gifts" at 8:00 P.M.

At that time in Shanghai it was dark, very dark. The leaves of the many poplar trees were dancing in the wind. There were no lights. The sound of the trucks and bicycles going by in the dark was eerie. Drivers maneuvered without their lights, flipping them on only when they thought there was something out there.

I have a little "chicken" in my blood and didn't want to go out on the street alone. I enlisted the services of Homer

Firestone, one of our group and previously a missionary to Bolivia. He met me at the door at eight o'clock. We walked out the side door, past the guard house where they said, "Good evening" to us in what seemed to be their newly acquired English, and on through the gate to the road outside.

On down the road a bit we stopped, waiting there in the shadows. Some trucks and bicycles went by in the dark. Only one flipped its lights at us. The dancing leaves on the poplars made the shadows eerie. It wasn't long before a bicycle came up to us. It was Mr. Pei.

This short Chinese man who spoke excellent English got off his bicycle and came closer. I realized that this was much better than the department store. Now we would have a little chance to talk. I asked him what he was doing there. He told me that his purpose was to get "the bread" to his people. They so needed "the bread of life" and there were no resources to get it for them. All the Bibles were burnt several years ago when Mao took over. He also told me that this was very dangerous for him. He had already been in prison three times for this and might go to prison again. "But," he added with conviction, "I have got to get the bread to our people and this is why I am taking these Bibles."

He was very nervous and did not tell me much more. He was anxious to be on his way. We had a short prayer together and then he left, speeding away on his bicycle in the dark. I knew I had just met a saint.

When I was getting those Bibles ready, I wrote a note that I slipped in with them telling him that I would be praying for him. I don't know why, but I also included my name and address.

The next morning my phone rang. It was Mr. Pei. He asked me if I lived in Franklin, Ohio, as my address had indicated. I told him that I did and then he wanted to know if I knew Jerry Back. Here we were in Shanghai, China and he was asking me if I knew someone in my hometown of twenty thousand people halfway around the world.

No, I didn't know him, but I asked him who this Jerry Back was. He said that he had a letter that he would like to send to Jerry. Would I take it? By now I was not only wanting to help, but intrigued as well. But this meant I needed to meet with him again. We were scheduled to have lunch at the DaNa Guest House just before our afternoon flight back to Hong Kong. I told him he could meet me there. I would be out in front waiting on him.

From our brief discussion the night before, I learned that a woman from the countryside was coming today to get some of the Bibles. I felt badly that I didn't have any money with me to give him for her bus fare. Now I could correct that. I went to our group and asked them for all their Chinese money to give to Mr. Pei. They gladly put it in my hand.

Our guide took us to lunch. I sent the group on into the dining room and headed for the street with my camera. You can certainly look like a tourist with a camera in hand and that is how I wanted to appear. Mr. Pei walked up to me and gave me the letter for Jerry Back and I gave him the money that I had collected from the group. He quickly told me that Jerry had brought him "gifts" earlier that year and he had a message for him. How amazing that here we were in Shanghai, half a world away from Franklin, Ohio, and there was this relationship.

My first "James Bond" adventure had turned out well in spite of my inexperience. Who would have ever guessed that that innocent trip of going into China would offer me those two wonderful adventures—talking with Wang about the Lord and delivering one hundred Bibles for Christians starved for the word of God?

The following year we went back to China, and this time Chuck was with me. We were able to take more Bibles. It was much easier for us but still very risky for Mr. Pei. Norma Koverman, one of our group, was with us, and since she was always taking pictures she got a good shot of Mr. Pei. This time Mr. Pei told us that he had received more than twenty thousand Bibles in circumstances like ours and had delivered them to Christians. What a privilege it was to help those Chinese Christians so hungry for the word of God. What an honor to meet a man, a saint, like Mr. Pei. How exciting that God turns adventure into ministry and ministry into adventure.

CHAPTER 13

SURROUNDED BY UNEXPECTED

SURPRISES: THE UNEXPECTED

Surprises? Yes. There is always something unexpected in ministry. How do you deal with it? Let the Lord tell you how.

A Stowaway

We had three surprises with the airplane that weren't expected. One was a couple of years after the Nicaragua earthquake. A work team near Managua completed rebuilding a church, a school, and some homes. As always, we mix with the local people.

The workcamp went great and the team was pleased but exhausted when they climbed on board our plane at the Managua airport for the flight home. Chester Lemmond, our team leader, and Bobbie Feiring, the stewardess on this trip, hustled everyone through immigration, got them on board, and settled down. Chuck and Jim Minor were piloting the plane that day so they were doing the last minute checklist, being sure all the paper work was complete. They filed the flight plan to New Orleans with a fuel stop on the way at Merida, Mexico. The fuel truck had just pulled away from our plane, so the tanks were full and it was time to go home.

"Bobbie, is everything ready on board? Do you have enough ice in the galley and did you get the sandwiches made for the trip?" Chuck called out.

"Everything's ready. Here is the passenger manifest and everyone is on board. Let's go home, I'm ready," she replied. Bobbie had worked hard on this trip. Usually our stewardess was also in charge of the food each day for our team. This was no easy task in a foreign country.

The door was closed and the baggage trucks pulled away from the plane. The left engine started with its beautiful sound, then the right. Looking out the window, the team waved again to all those friends from Nicaragua who had come to see them off. There was Misael and Amina Lopez, Ali Velasquez, Hermano Felipe, and countless others. Those dear friends would never let our teams leave without being at the airport and sending them off with their prayers and their love.

The plane taxied down past the hangars to the end of the runway, then Chuck stopped for prayer. Prayer before take-off had been placed on the checklist when we first bought the plane, and it was considered as important as checking the fuel tanks. After the "amen," he pushed the throttle forward and the engines began their roar as the plane started picking up speed rolling down the runway. Chuck yelled, "rotate," and the wheels left the cement with the nose rising and then leveling off. "Gear up" was the next call by Chuck, and they gained altitude. *Going home after a rewarding two weeks of helping our new Christian friends recover from their earthquake feels good,* Chuck thought to himself.

When the seat belt sign went off, Bobbie got up to check the galley again and start serving drinks. Seemed like the ice chest was out in the way this time. What was wrong? Giving it a shove, she tried to get it back in place, but it wouldn't go. That was strange. Why wouldn't it go back in where it belonged? She shoved again, and since it wouldn't move, she pulled it forward to see what could be behind it.

There was somebody back there! She saw someone's head. Turning on her heels, she headed for the cockpit to tell Chuck. This was frightening. There were so many hijackings lately. They were in the newspapers all the time. Was this what this was? She half-ran up the aisle, opened the cockpit door and yelled, "Chuck, there is someone in the galley behind the ice chest. I don't know who it is and what he is there for. Is this a hijacking? What shall I do?"

Chuck started to get up to go back there but then he reconsidered. They had better tell "Managua radio" what was going on first. He picked up his microphone. "Managua radio, this is Convair 90844."

"Convair 90844 this is Managua radio, go ahead."

"We've got a problem. There is an extra person on board. We don't know who he is or why he is here but it has caused us alarm."

"90844, stand by."

"Bobbie, you just stay up here until we have orders from Managua radio. This could be one of those hijackings. There was one last week in California. But then again, maybe it's not," Chuck was thinking out loud now.

"90844, this is Managua radio. You are requested to return to the Managua airport. We will meet your plane. It is best if you do not cause any alarm at this time. Just gently turn your plane to return to the airport."

"Yes, sir. We will do that. However, we have full tanks of fuel and are not able to land with that load. Please advise." Chuck was busy trying to figure out how best to get the plane back down.

"90844, go ahead and burn off what fuel you feel is necessary before descending. We will monitor your position and will stay on this radio frequency to monitor any activity. Where is this person now?"

"He is in the galley at the back of the plane. We don't know anything about him, only that he is on board." Chuck explained.

"It would be best if you keep everything as normal as possible. How long do you think it will take to burn off the fuel?" Managua radio asked.

"We have started circling, but it will probably be twenty-five or thirty minutes before we can land. Are there any known problems like this in this area?" Chuck's mind was reeling, considering all the possibilities.

"Bobbie," Chuck said, "Go back and talk to the passengers and try to keep them from getting up. Just talk with them and be friendly but keep an eye on the galley. Don't go to the galley. And keep me informed the minute you see anything more."

It seemed hours before the fuel was down enough to land, but it was done in twenty-five minutes. Chuck and Jim brought the plane down so carefully that the passengers didn't know they were landing until they were over the runway and the wheels were ready to touch the ground.

Jumping from the cockpit, both Chuck and Jim nearly threw the stairs down. The airport police were right there and raced up the steps. Looking over the passengers, one stayed at the front and the other hurried to the galley with Bobbie right behind. Pulling out the ice chest, they saw him. It was a man. No, it was a boy. A very frightened little boy in his early teens.

The officer pulled him out and, as he stumbled to his feet, started asking him questions. "What are you doing here? What do you want? How did you get on board this airplane? What is your purpose?"

Not waiting for answers, he shoved him on ahead of him down the aisle to the door. The other officer half carried him down the stairs where they could interrogate him further.

Now the workcampers were full of questions. "What's happening?" they asked. Chuck and Jim were there on the tarmac with the police. It was Bobbie's job to explain all of this. Crowding to look out the windows on that side of the plane, they could see that this was a teenager. They recognized him.

"Hey, it's Miguel." He was one of the boys from where the group was working. He was with them nearly everyday as they were laying block and rebuilding the church that the earthquake had destroyed. What in the world was going on?

Chuck, seeing that it was Miguel, said, "Miguel, what in the world are you doing on our plane?"

"I wanted to go with you. I don't have any place to live here and my parents were killed in the earthquake, and you all were so kind to me. I just want to stay with you. Can I go with you?" Miguel pleaded.

"Oh, Miguel, Miguel. I am so sorry. Don't you have a home

to go to? Where have you been living? You can't just leave like this." Chuck was overcome with the possibilities of this situation.

"Miguel, we were so happy to have you with us while we were working. You helped us a lot and you were a great interpreter too. But Miguel, you just can't hide in our plane and go back to the United States with us. No matter how much we want to take you, your government won't allow it and we can't get you into the United States like this. When we land in New Orleans, they would put you on the first plane back to Nicaragua and certainly not allow you to stay. Then there would also be a huge fine on us for bringing you with us. I am so sorry. We wish we could help you. We wish we could take you home with us but it just isn't possible." Chuck tried to explain.

The workcampers had come down the stairs and gathered around to hear what was going on. They were bewildered too, searching for some way to help Miguel.

The police were ready to take him back into the airport when Chuck spoke up.

"Sir, let us have a minute with Miguel and then I'll bring him to you. We want to talk with him and have prayer with him before we leave again. Okay?"

As the two policemen moved off, the group was really disturbed because they didn't want to leave him there, although they really had no choice. Then Chester said, "Let's give him some money so he can get some help and some food when he goes back. Come on, guys. See what money you have in your pockets."

That wasn't the solution they wanted, but it was a solution. They were able to give Miguel some money, pray with him, tell him to go see Misael Lopez and he would help him, and then Chuck took him over to the policemen.

Reboarding the plane, the group was very somber. It seemed each one was trying to find some way to help Miguel, some way to get him to the States. Some were even thinking, *What if that was my child?* They watched as the police led him inside before sending him back to his village. Then Chuck and Jim climbed back in the cockpit and started the flight home again.

We inquired about Miguel at the next workcamp, about two months later. He was doing fine. Misael found an older couple that could take him to live with them. Chester especially searched for him. Miguel was delighted that he remembered him and looked him up. As he told Misael later, "See, my American friends didn't forget me."

Fixed Bayonets and Machine Guns

I wasn't really sure what a bayonet looked like. I never saw one up close. But there were soldiers around our plane with machine guns and what must be bayonets attached to their guns. It looked like twenty or so soldiers out there and they were looking at the cockpit window and calling to Chuck and Jerry Cunningham (our first officer) to open the door of our plane and let them in.

We were in Mexico City for our first stop on this EyeWitness trip. There were forty people with us and we went to Cuernavaca for a Christian World Conference. Leaving there around 3:00 P.M., we planned to arrive in Guatemala City before dark. But that was not to be. Thunderstorms were right in our path, and as we approached Guatemala we had to make our way around them. The wind was bumping us around as we got closer to the storm when Guatemala radio told Jerry that their airport was closed. There were only two alternative airports— Puerto San Jose or Puerto Barrio. Puerto San Jose was on the Pacific coast south of Guatemala City but it was a military base and not open to civilian planes. Puerto Barrio was much further away on the Caribbean side. Chuck and Jerry knew they had to choose one of these airports because their fuel supply wouldn't allow them to go on to El Salvador or back to Mexico. Since Puerto San Jose was closer, they told Guatemala radio they would be landing there.

They called the tower radio at Puerto San Jose but no one answered. They could see the waves in the Pacific Ocean even in the darkness, but they had trouble finding the runway. Jerry was checking out the beach to see if they could land on it if necessary. The darkness and lightning of the thunderstorm was to the north now. Chuck kept trying to get the tower to answer but there was no response. We needed to land there somehow, and we sure didn't want to land on the beach. That would be dangerous and do damage to the plane. Then Jerry spotted the runway at the base. There were no lights on it but they could see it well enough to land. Making the approach and turning on the final path, they still kept trying to get the tower to respond but it was silent, deathly silent. Where were they? Why didn't they answer? And why weren't there lights down there?

It was an uneventful landing. They greased the wheels on the runway as if they could see it very well. Now what? There was a small light over in the distance on the right. Maybe that was where the control tower was. Maybe we can find someone over there and wait out the storm in Guatemala City.

Jerry started taxiing the plane in that direction when two military trucks came speeding up, blocking our path and stopping right in front of our plane. It wasn't hard to know that we were supposed to stop

A tall man, who must have been their Captain, called to Jerry. Jerry pushed his window open as the man was telling him to open the door to the plane. Chuck jumped from his seat and called to Luz to help him. Luz Gonzales, a Mexican pastor and our friend, was with us as our interpreter. As Chuck opened the door and let the stairs down, Luz started down to find out what was going on. He only got about halfway when he turned around and ran back up the stairs yelling, "Chuck, they've got guns down there. There are machine guns and bayonets. There are a lot of soldiers."

During that decade there had been many hijackings in Latin America and actually the whole Western Hemisphere. This made the authorities at Puerto San Jose skeptical about our landing there and concerned as to what was on the plane. They thought it was another hijacking and were ready to deal with us with military force. Chuck went down the stairs rather slowly so he could take in the whole situation. He must explain to them who we were and why we were there.

"Sir, this is a church airplane. We were on our way to Guatemala City but a thunderstorm there prevented us from landing. Radio Guatemala told us to land at either Puerto San Jose or Puerto Barrio and we chose here." They weren't convinced.

The Captain barked out, "Get everyone off the plane. Have them stand right there under the wing—together—now!"

Chuck hurried back up the stairs. "Okay, everyone get off the plane. The officer wants us all off and to stand under the wing on this side of the plane. We want to do exactly what he says. Stay together. They want to check us out and see what we have on board. Don't worry. Everything will be all right. Donna, you stay on board and show them what they want to see." Chuck was tense as he led the group down the stairs. They each got up very quickly and followed him down.

Two of the soldiers, still with their machine guns and bayonets, started up the stairs. I waited for them but they didn't pay any attention to me. They went right to the cockpit searching that area. Next they inspected the front storage area and coat rack. They looked it over very carefully. Then they approached the seats, looking them over thoroughly, underneath, and in the seat pockets, then the overhead rack. They moved some of the things around that our people left and didn't bother putting them back. I stayed with them but mostly out of their way unless they motioned for me when they found something a little unusual. They didn't find anything really and seemed a bit disappointed and surprised. I didn't know what they were looking for but later I realized it was probably drugs.

Motioning for me to follow them, we went down the stairs and I joined the group under the wing. The two soldiers went over to the Captain and started talking. I am sure they were reporting that they didn't find anything. The rest of the soldiers encircled our group and stood there with their machine guns and fixed bayonets like they were ready for something. After a few minutes but it seemed forever, the Captain walked over to Chuck and questioned again, "What kind of plane is this?"

Chuck repeated, "It's a church airplane. We came from

Mexico where we were at a church meeting and we're going to Guatemala City to visit some churches there."

The Captain's voice softened. "Well, okay, but I don't think you can make it tonight. What do you want to do now?" The soldiers had put their guns away and the atmosphere was beginning to feel much friendlier.

"Is there a place we can go?" Chuck asked. "I need to call Guatemala City and see how we can get these people there. We have reservations at the Pan American Hotel. How far is it from here?

"It's about two hours by bus. You'll need to get a bus I suppose. You can bring your people on over to our hangar. There is room there for everyone and a phone you can use. We've got these two army trucks. They can take your women and the luggage. Your men can walk." The Captain began to be accommodating.

Chuck shared this information with the group. Our men got busy unloading the luggage from the plane and the women went back on board the plane to collect the items they left in their hurry to disembark. They didn't have any steps or ladders and those truck beds were about four feet off the ground. It wasn't going to be easy to get up in those trucks. We ended up with the men using their hands clasped together for a makeshift ladder. Our group was working as a great team.

Arriving at the hangar, each one was checking to see if they had all of their luggage and bags. It was simply a hangar. No chairs, no tables. There was no food around there either. We realized there wasn't going to be any supper tonight. We knew we had a diabetic with us, so we started pulling out crackers, candy, oranges, bananas, cheese, all kinds of snacks to be sure he ate. Surprisingly enough, he not only ate but since we were now sharing there was enough for everyone. It was sort of like the little boy and his loaves and fishes when Jesus fed the five thousand. We too had some leftovers.

They led Chuck off to the only telephone around there and now he came hurrying in the door. "Well, we have good news and we have bad news. The good news is that we have a bus coming to take you to Guatemala City. The bad news is that it has to come from Guatemala City to get you and that will take a couple of hours. Jerry and I will stay with the plane and fly it up in the morning. I have called the hotel and they will be waiting for you. So now it's just a matter of waiting for the bus."

What does a group of Christians do when they have time on their hands? We joined hands forming a circle. We sang at the conference in Mexico, so we had lots of songs we enjoyed. It was calming and relaxing to sing after the stress of the flight and now being here in the hangar. The soldiers followed us in but were pretty much keeping their distance. Most of them were together over by a small plane parked in the corner. However, as our singing continued, they gradually moved closer. It wasn't too long before those of our group closest to a soldier reached out their hands and brought them into our circle.

Right in the middle of all of this I remembered another time when our plane was not welcome. It was a good time to tell them about it. Might make them more comfortable in these circumstances. "Chuck, remember the time we were the pawn between Mexico and the United States. Why don't you tell them about that?"

"Hey team," Chuck called out. "Let me tell you about another time somewhat like what we are going through tonight. You all know where Merida, Mexico, is as we fueled there on our way down here. We'll be fueling there on our way home this time, too.

"Well, in 1974 when we had the first fuel crunch because of the policies of the Middle East oil-producing countries, we found ourselves right in the middle of a problem. It was a routine trip, that is if any of our trips are routine. We had about thirty-six people in that group and were working in Guatemala building a church in Tecpan. We plan to show you that church while we are down here. The church people there appreciated our help so much and we developed a great friendship in those two weeks we were working together. You'll see them and they'll have a special service for us this trip.

"Well, we took off from Guatemala City around eight o'clock that morning heading north. Merida was the first stop and then we were to go to New Orleans and home. The mood was jovial as we landed. We know that airport as we use it on all of our trips down here. It is perfect for these over-the-gulf flights.

"Our crew this time was Dick Sanders and Don Shaver. These experienced pilots knew this airport and knew exactly what it took to get fuel and to be off again for the next leg. But this time it was different. Instead of the fuel truck coming up, it was a military jeep much like tonight.

"It was late morning, and the heat really comes off that tarmac in the middle of the day in Mexico. Dick told me that they let down the stairs and some of the group was already down by the time Dick got down there to check with the jeep and ask about the fuel truck.

"To make a long story short, the officer told Dick that they weren't going to fuel our plane. The reason was that several Mexican planes brought their passengers to American airports on their scheduled flights and the Americans had refused to completely fill their tanks, only giving them enough fuel to return to Mexico. They considered this an insult and were going to get even, using us and our plane this time. Here we were caught between two countries, Mexico and the United States, and in this awkward relationship. Not a great position to be in.

"Dick called us back in Wichita and told us the dilemma. Now we had to figure out a way to get those people home. We put in a call to Enrique Cepeda, our Mexican friend who was pastor of a church in Mexico City, asking him for help. Enrique got busy and I don't know how he did it but he got to the right people. That was a miracle in itself. He got them to change their mind and to contact the Merida airport authorities with instructions to give Dick the fuel he had to have to get the plane on home. Now, of course, you know there was prayer involved in this too. All together from the time Dick found out he had a problem, until he had the fuel was about an eleven hour delay. But they made it off to New Orleans and on home, praising the Lord for answered prayer all the way.

"Now does this story have some similarity to what we have been dealing with tonight?" Chuck summed up the incident.

About that time the bus arrived, so we got busy finding our luggage, loading it, and preparing for the midnight ride. Of course, we made it to Guatemala City that night even though we were bone weary when we finally arrived at the hotel. It wasn't until breakfast in the hotel the next morning when we seemed to realize the adventure of the night before. Imagine—being in a plane that landed at a military base in Guatemala and being met with fixed bayonets and machine guns. What a story to tell when we got home. Life is full of surprises for us, but not for the Lord.

CHAPTER 14
PRAISE: RECALLING THE LORD'S BENEFITS

Shortly after Chuck was healed from his heart problem I received an idea. With that healing, plus all the great things that the Lord was doing for us at Project Partner it was apparent to me that I needed some new way to thank him. What could we do that was special?

I chose March 14 as the day we would set aside each year to honor him. We would come to the office as usual, but it would be a special day. We would spend the day in worship, in praise, and in thanksgiving.

Does the Lord want us to thank him? Does the Lord want us to remember the things he does for us? It seems to me that obedience, praise, and appreciation are what please him.

Circulating a note to all the staff, we asked for their input on how the Lord answered prayer in their life and our ministry. When we put these together, we compiled quite a list of blessings from the Lord. With these we then wrote a litany recalling many of the blessings and answers the Lord gave us that past year. We assigned different staff members to speak about the blessings that were most important in their lives and work. We planned a lunch together and a period of prayer followed by a Communion service. Spouses were invited to come for the day.

March 14 was indeed a special day of praise. It became a tradition, something that we looked forward to each year.

It is easy to get so caught up in the day-to-day activities and problems that we lose our praise, our joy, and our perspective. After losing Chuck and then losing Project Partner for a while, I came to the realization that joy is something we have to choose. Happiness is a continual pursuit. Joy is a gift from God. Paul tells us, "Rejoice in the Lord always, and again I say rejoice." It is a choice.

Remembering His Promises

I remember the morning I first went back to Project Partner after it was returned to me. The keys were delivered to me at my house at 5:00 P.M. on December 31 with the instruction that the security code would be changed at midnight. I chose January 2, 1994, to go to the office and begin my first day as president of a new Project Partner.

The key worked in the door. The security code turned off the signal. I looked around cautiously. I hadn't been there for almost a year and a half. The place was so quiet. Nobody was there. The desks were clean, the chairs were placed where they should be, and the trash was emptied. A lot of things had been moved in the months I was gone. Walking through each room was a bit eerie. Very little was like I had left it. I searched to find out how to start over.

It was overwhelming. I asked Steve Parson, who recently retired from the Air Force in recovery management, to help me. He arrived not long after I did. So there were the two of us, trying to pick up where eighteen people were working.

Starting with the computers, I discovered that I didn't know the codes. They were changed. I started to call our software consultant only to discover that I didn't know the codes to use the telephone either. I couldn't make a long distance call without them. Where were the files that gave that information?

The phone rang. A woman wanted some information on one of the Agape children in Guatemala. I didn't know where that file was. I didn't even know which room it was in. How could I possibly find the answer? Nobody to ask. Nobody was there who knew the answer. Just Steve and me. Time for a choice.

I told the woman that I didn't have that information right now but would call her back. I told Steve that I was leaving for a bit but would be back shortly. I walked out of the office and drove to the church where a couple of my friends were counting the church offering that Monday morning. I told them of my frustrations and the problems, and I asked them to pray with me that I could get the Lord's direction and have joy in my heart. This was not the time for discouragement because I knew the Lord placed me back there. It was a time for praise and rejoicing. But I had an immediate problem and undoubtedly many more would come up. It was a time for prayer.

That did it. The Lord was with me. Now I had his joy. It didn't matter if I knew the codes at the moment. I knew I would find them sometime. It didn't matter if I didn't have all the answers. The Lord was with me and he would help me find the answers in his time. It certainly gave me a peace and assurance that I desperately needed.

Then I remembered again the message that the Lord gave me in 1993, the day after the board told me that I could have Project Partner back. That day I took Samuel Stephens to the Cincinnati airport for his flight back to India and delivered Enrique Cepeda to the church he was supposed to speak at in Columbus. I was on my way home when God's special message came to me. "My child, why do you doubt? I will take care of you. I have my plans for you. I have plans to prosper you and not to harm you." I wrote it down. I didn't ever want to forget it. I wanted every word just as it came to me.

If the Lord gave me that message on October 29, 1993, why would I think he would not be with me on January 2, 1994? Or any time for that matter? His affirmation is that he will *indeed* take care of me regardless. There isn't any condition in those words. They are just there … and with no ending. Ah, yes. What a joy to remember God's promises!

But the Lord wasn't finished taking care of me. He has his plans. He knew that I could only do so much back in the office and that I would need to train someone to replace me in time. I needed to provide a legacy so that this ministry would not die with me but would continue on, grow, change, develop and do God's will God's way.

It was eighteen months later that the Lord brought Robert Gregory across my path. He seemed like a nice young man and although he brought great educational credentials and was offered a much more lucrative job, he was willing to help me temporarily. Working in the office, he soon saw the scope of the ministry—that we worked with extremely productive national leaders who were reaching hundreds of thousands for Christ in their own country. He saw that together, we were making a significant difference in several countries in this world. He saw that this ministry would provide purpose and direction for his life.

As the weeks and months went by, Robert kept asking questions, studying about these countries, praying for the national leaders, and developing a love and joy in the work. It wasn't long before he told me, "Donna, I think this is where the Lord wants me to be. He has placed this ministry on my heart and I want to do whatever it takes to serve him here and to help you with all that is going on."

That was a joy to hear! It certainly wasn't the salary that brought him. As I watched him, I saw that he believed in the core values of Project Partner. He understood the concepts, agreed that this was a unique ministry that the Lord gave us, and wanted to dedicate his life to it. There were still times of testing which he endured, and on November 12, 1998, he was commissioned as the president of Project Partner and challenged to take the ministry on in new ways that only God knew and would disclose to him.

This rang the bell of praise in my heart. Yes, I wanted to continue in this work the rest of my life, but I needed someone to pick up the torch and carry it on. The Lord provided and provided well. Just as Joshua replaced Moses, Solomon replaced David, Elisha replaced Elijah, and on through Bible history, I knew that the Lord needed to replace me so the work could go on. I praise the Lord for providing.

He certainly knows the path ahead and prepares the way. He did it this time by bringing Robert Gregory in to move the work that Chuck and I started into a new millennium.

Unexpected Results

Sometimes recalling God's promises happens in most unusual ways. There was only one reason I was in Asia in April of 1985 and not home with Chuck, and that was because of that church building that Pastor Loo built in China. I didn't want to miss the dedication. I carried the final check to complete my commitment for the construction costs in my pocket.

Our team for this trip arrived in Hong Kong the day before and spent most of the time getting Chinese visas. I thought it would be simple but it took all day, mostly just waiting. It was more than a bit unusual to admit a group such as ours into Communist China. At 5:30 that afternoon the China Tourist Bureau handed our passports back to us with our visas stamped inside. We could go into China.

The next morning at 7:00 A.M. we caught the bus to the Star Ferry. Arthur Gee, the man who had introduced me to Pastor Loo, and Arthur's secretary, Esther, met us there. There were always tremendous numbers of people lined up for the ferry, and that morning was no exception. When the gates opened to let the passengers on board, it reminded me of opening a gate on my grandfather's farm for a herd of cattle to come in. There are so many people in Asia.

It didn't take long to cross the harbor, but then we taxied to the Far East Jetfoil pier. Arthur purchased our tickets and led us through immigration and customs. Finally we were seated on the Jetfoil at 8:30 for the hour-long trip to Macau.

Pastor Loo was waiting for us as we came out of immigration in Macau. We loaded into his van and he drove us right to the gate into mainland China, parked the van, and we walked across to the Chinese immigration and customs. This time permission to enter took longer and there was lots of paper work, but by 10:15 we were on the other side and into a van Pastor Loo hired there.

We drove through the city and into the countryside. It was certainly China. How could I forget? Many of the people, both men and women, still wore the blue uniforms of the Communist regime. There were people everywhere you looked. Laborers were building the road by carrying two baskets of dirt on their shoulders, one on each end of a stick for balance. It is not a quick process to build a road like that in China. How long does that take? Who was in a hurry anyway?

We came to ponds—it seemed hundreds of duck ponds—one after another with ducks of all sizes. The baby ducks were obediently following their mothers. There were rice patties and garden plots. Honking the horn was a practice everyone participated in. When the road narrowed to about a lane and a half, the horn was used continually.

We were in the economic free zone, so there was much more enterprise here than in the rest of China. And more cars, vehicles, and strange little tractors pulling various wagonloads of things. Lots of bicycles, of course. And lots of people walking in all directions.

We arrived at a town and went on to a cemetery gate. We could see a tall Buddhist pagoda up on the left and burial sites under and around it. We headed to the right of it through the trees: pine, hemlock, apple, and pear. Finally, we drove up to the new church. It looked great, although a bit smaller than I imagined. Red brick, stained glass windows, tile roof, and on the right were cemetery plots. It was ten long steps to the door up from the street, rock construction up to the window level, and then brick. The windows were gothic shaped, and there was a cross on the front above the door. At the back of the sanctuary on each side was a twelve-by-twelve-foot room, the right one was an office, the left one was a lavatory.

Outside to the right of the building were a monument and a cross. Fourteen students from the Bible school were present. This dedication service was to be for the workers, the ones who actually built the building. The church was called the Christian Chapel, and was to be used as a training center and meeting place for Christians in this area. There were more than a million people living within twenty miles of the facility.

The construction workers arrived on their lunch hour. Pastor Loo told them to come and he would supply their lunch. They didn't know yet that the building was a church, and they certainly didn't know that a dedication ceremony would take place during their lunchtime. The Bible school students brought the workers inside and up to the chairs at the front. There was a large table of food over at the left to add to the celebration.

Pastor Loo started the service with singing. The students passed out programs with the words to the songs. Pastor Loo taught these songs to the workers and, of course, the Bible school students helped. It was obvious that the workers were the honored guests. Pastor Loo was very energetic with real charisma. After the songs, he changed the mood by explaining that the building they worked on was a church. He told them why it was built, who Jesus Christ is, and what he could do for everyone. Then it was my turn.

With Esther as my interpreter, I started with the question that Wang had asked me in 1981 back in Beijing on my first visit to China, "Does your religion help you with your problems?" I continued by telling them why Jesus was important to me, how he could bring them peace, joy, and happiness, and that he could give them eternal life. This is the message everyone needs to hear.

After I finished, Pastor Loo went to the table and picked up a plate of chicken, bringing it back over to the pulpit. He explained that God is the giver of good things and of life, and that we could enjoy this food because of God's plan. We would thank God for it before we ate. Prayer was new to the workers, and they awkwardly bowed their heads, but I'm not sure they closed their eyes. After his prayer, the students took a plate of food to each of the workers.

It was equivalent to a picnic except it was in the church. The chicken was boiled instead of fried. There were hard-boiled eggs, buns, rolls with sausages inside, and cola in cans. Those twenty-five or thirty workers were really loaded down with food. The students kept bringing them more and more. The worker sitting behind me whispered something to Esther. She later told me he said, "Who is this Jesus? I've never heard of him before. How can I find out more about him?"

After that enormous lunch, the students cleaned everything up and we went outside for pictures. The workers liked the idea of pictures. They lined up eagerly like young schoolboys with each trying to see who could be in front. Too bad I didn't have a Polaroid camera so each one of them could have taken a picture home that day.

As Pastor Loo, Esther, and I stood at the monument outside the church and I gave Pastor Loo my final check of $2,000, which completed my pledge to him for this building, he began to tell me more about his work and his plans and goals. This really made my head swim. I never dreamed this small church would be used in so many different ways.

This church building would be much more than a church. It would be a training center to bring in house church leaders and workers for classes in evangelism and discipleship. Pastor Loo trains his people in house-to-house, person-to-person evangelism. Then they can bring new believers to the church for discipleship, "gospel tea times," program meetings, picnics, and such. He would also use this church to bring in house church leaders from across the Guangdong province and the other three provinces where he was working at that time—Hainan, Wanzhou, and Fukien.

Pastor Loo went on to tell me that there were three hundred fifty house church leaders and more than two thousand house churches. (I had to make Esther repeat this because it sounded so great.) Already he was directly and indirectly responsible for more than two hundred thousand Christians. I couldn't believe my ears. His role, he explained, was to train, plan, and strategize with the leaders, and to see that they got the materials and financial support they needed.

I was greatly impressed with all of this. Never in a million years did I dream that the Lord would give me this fantastic opportunity to help get the Gospel to so many in China. My mind went back to that morning three years earlier when, in Tiananmen Square in Beijing, my heart was broken for those people who were staring at me—those people who knew nothing about Jesus Christ. Here was the Lord's answer to that moment. He gave me the burden for the Chinese and then he gave me the way to participate with them learning about Jesus Christ and his power to change lives.

Pastor Loo said that one of the areas growing the fastest was near Shanghai, where many previous Western missionaries were and where Watchman Nee did his ministry. They could easily get one hundred more leaders here and two hundred more there if they had the funds for transportation, materials, and a place for training. It was easy to tell that Pastor Loo's heart was for China. So many had never heard of Jesus, and Pastor Loo's purpose was to change that.

We said good-bye to the workers and the students. They were still waving to us as we pulled away in the van. Looking back at those waving hands, I was overcome with the knowledge that the Lord's plans are perfect, and what a tremendous joy it is to be included.

Our trip was put in reverse as we went back to the border, through the Chinese immigration and customs, walking across the border, and into Macau where that van was waiting. After tea at a coffee shop, we left Macau on the Jetfoil for the ride back to Hong Kong, a tired, happy, dirty, fulfilled, challenged, pleased, motivated, and overwhelmed bunch.

Praise is our response to God. It is our way of saying "Thank you." That day's praise went something like this: "Thank you, Father, for directing our paths and using us for your purposes. Thank you for allowing us to make a difference in China."

CHAPTER 15

OPPORTUNITIES: LOOKING AT OPTIONS

There are times we are a bit discontent. We are ready for a new adventure, looking for just the right mountain. We need a challenge with significance. The Lord uses these times to move us on, get us out of our rut, and prepare us to tackle a new challenge.

Choosing Carefully

In 1993 I was asked to go with a team of fifteen to Russia to see about developing a program to help a church there. The door was wide open for Christian work. A major American pastor was exploring the possibility of spreading his television ministry to Russia, and he wanted me to be in a group that would help him assess the opportunities.

I was the only one who had traveled to Moscow before. It seemed as if everyone in the group was afraid of everything—from eating away from the hotel to walking the streets or using the subway. Their fear caused me to feel hemmed in. I tried to be patient, because I remembered my first trip there and my first Rio Grande.

According to the program, we met with some Russian Orthodox pastors and leaders to see how we could be of benefit. This included a trip some fifty miles or so to village churches where they showed us a farm commune and then spread a picnic for us with the Orthodox clergy. They later held an impressive meeting with government leaders for us in their White House, as well as hosting us at special dinners and escorting us through Moscow like VIPs.

In the end, I decided this venture wasn't for me, even though I was searching very hard at the time to do something of significance. The Lord showed me that serving national leaders and enabling them to reach out to their own people was a powerful way to do effective ministry. This group's philosophy ran counter to mine. They wanted to help the nationals, but they also wanted to control and run the program in Russia. I knew that was not the way the Lord wanted me to work with him, so there was no way that I could participate in their plans without compromising my own beliefs. This mountain wasn't for me. I'd have to keep looking.

A Time for Change

There was a time for our boat, Sea Angel, and there was a time when it was not productive. Things change. God leads us with divine discontent in knowing when to change, rather than hanging on to the past.

One of the most difficult changes that I had to make was discontinuing work camps. We took work teams for fifteen years. The groups and the people we ministered to were so loved by each other. And the participants loved the journey. Each trip was productive. We built many churches in all the countries of Central America, and some in South America. But a day came to move on. The Lord was leading us in a new direction. The hardest part of this change was telling our constituents that we were no longer going to be doing these projects. When people would write or call about the next workcamp, I found it very difficult to tell them. Methods change. And the Lord uses those changes for his good.

Starting something new is more exciting than stopping a program. When the idea of a "mission cruise" in the Caribbean came to us, it sounded like fun. It would be productive, too. In January of 1977 we sponsored our first one. I negotiated with a cruise ship to take sixty-five people. We used the ports of Cap Haitien, Puerta Plata, San Juan, and St. Thomas for an introduction to missions. It worked well, so we sponsored another in

1978 and another in 1979. As ideas grew, we decided to charter a whole ship. That was a huge undertaking, and it involved signing a cruise ship contract for more than $500,000.

We were able to get some very special leadership that made the cruise very attractive. Dr. Dale Oldham was our main speaker. Our music was provided by Doug Oldham and Sandy Patti. Teams from different states helped us with all the programming and logistics. The Lord blessed this effort, and we filled every room on board that ship as we sailed out of Miami harbor on January 16, 1980. It was a huge success and a great time to remember.

The purpose of this cruise was to show people the mission work going on in Jamaica, Haiti, and the Dominican Republic. During the years we took work teams to those countries, so we had a great relationship with the nationals. The cruise ship allowed us to take more than a forty-passenger plane could hold. There were five hundred sixty-four people on that cruise ship, and everyone of them got to see the work of the Lord and fellowship with the believers in Kingston, Port au Prince, and Puerta Plata. It was a unique experience, a new way of doing things, and another opportunity to make more people aware and concerned for the work of the Lord in other countries.

We made one *big* mistake. I made it first. We were docked in Kingston, Jamaica. Some of our Jamaican friends asked if they could go on board and see the ship. "Sure," I replied, "I'll show you around." They were intrigued with the cabins and berths, and they loved the stairs and the lounges. The great entertainment hall made their eyes light up, they had never seen anything like this before.

Then I opened the door to the dining room. Immediately I knew I made a mistake. The staff was preparing the food for the midnight buffet. Typical of most cruise ships, this midnight buffet was lavish. All kinds of food adorned the tables, and everything you can think of, including fancy ice carvings, decorated the feast on either end of the buffet. I tried to turn the group around, but they caught a glimpse and scurried around me so fast that I was now at the back of the group. They wanted to see this. Their eyes were big. They were leaning over the rail just drinking in the beauty of all that food. They were even taking big breaths to enjoy the smells as well as the sights.

These people were lucky to have three scant meals a day. They had just come from a socialistic society back into a democracy. Just getting food on the table was a difficult task. Here we "rich Americans" received three great meals and then something this lavish at midnight. To them, this was hard to fathom. I felt ashamed and embarrassed, first that so much food was prepared for us, and then because they saw it and couldn't have any. This beautiful, lavish buffet was not for them. I would have given anything to shield them from this, or better yet, to have invited them in to eat.

As I was finally heading them toward the door to leave, Chuck made the same mistake with another group who asked for a tour. This was an unforgettable experience to see all that food, and for us to be so embarrassed about our affluence. The Lord showed us something important, and we made changes in the upcoming trips

Another opportunity that came our way for a while was working with college-aged people. We put together a program called "Classroom Without Walls," and working with Warner Southern College in Florida, we took their students for a term overseas. We did this first in Guatemala, later in Mexico, and then Germany. On those trips, students lived among the people, studied their history and culture, and saw how Christianity impacted their lives.

The cruises were right, for a time. Classroom Without Walls filled a need, for a time. The medical boat, Sea Angel served a distinct purpose. The workcamps were always good. Everything had its time. We made choices and followed the Lord's guidance. The Lord changed our focus in his time, moving us from the good in one choice to a better way and then another.

The key to opportunities is God's vision. He has more mountains out there for us. We have to discern his guidance, learn to listen for God's will, and go his way. My impatience sometimes wins out when I should be taking the time to seek God's guidance and be sure each new mountain is what he wants for me at the time. I'm still learning this lesson.

Bringing Churches Together for Kingdom Work

WIP was definitely a new mountain. WIP is the Wichita India Project, and it began in 1995 as an inspiration of what might be possible. It was yet another new way of "doing missions" we felt led to explore. I learned to love finding these new ways and taking the challenge and risk to see what can happen.

Chuck and I continued to travel to Wichita fairly often after we moved to Ohio, because the churches and people there continued to work with us. We were still a part of their missions outreach and they were part of ours. A small group of missions leaders began to gather monthly for lunch and to get updates on other missions projects. They invited me to one of their lunches. I brought Samuel Stephens with me.

After Samuel shared what the Lord was doing in India, I asked these mission leaders if they would be interested in doing an India project together. They could take a region and enable the Indian pastors to reach that region for Christ. "Sure," they said, "Send us a proposal and we'll see what we can do."

To my knowledge, this concept of a joint church project was previously unattempted. I didn't have any pattern to follow. Returning to India, Samuel sent me the basic information I needed and chose the Periyar region, a county of more than two million Hindu people with no knowledge of Christ. My job would be to get these churches and others of various denominations across Wichita working together for this one project. This was certainly a new mountain, and a mountain of work.

Three key church leaders, Larry Wren of Westlink Christian Church, David Bridgman of Eastminster Presbyterian, and Ron Grover, of Central Christian Church, believed in the idea and were ready to start work on the project. After I presented the first proposal, they kindly told me that it was too bulky and involved.

The second proposal seemed workable. We decided the best way to start was for them to make appointments for me at churches across town and for me to go out and "sell" the program.

At the first interview I fielded the question, "What is the next step and how will we work all this out?" I didn't have an answer in my head but knew I needed a response.

"Well, we will have a workshop to explain the process, to hear about the people and culture, discuss the need and the goal, and finally to outline how you and your congregation can have a major part in bringing Christ to these people. This is July. How about September 12? We could use Westlink Christian Church facilities. Would you be able to come?" Their answer was yes. Other churches agreed as well. Our plan was well underway.

The date was set, the workshop plans began, and we moved in that direction. I made calls on twenty churches and had twenty positive responses. That was tremendously encouraging, even though some of them couldn't carry through with their desire to be a part. Interest continued to grow and develop as more contacts were made into an ever-increasing group of Wichita churches.

I had put together an eighteen-page plan for the first workshop and was praying that morning as the group assembled. This whole idea for WIP depended on the workshop's success and on the leaders seeing the potential that they could really make a difference in India. We started with information about the area, the Periyar Region in Tamil Nadu, South India. I had a map of Kansas and Sedgwick County, where Wichita is located. I superimposed the Periyar Region on top of that, showing them that it was basically the same size as Sedgwick County.

Sedgwick County has a population of well beyond three hundred thousand, but Periyar has more than two million people, about the same as all of Kansas. The plan called for WIP to provide prayer support, financial support of $245,000 during a three year period, and participate directly by sending their pastors to lead some conferences for the pastors in India. The India Gospel League and its teams of "barefoot pastors" would reach across the Periyar Region and in three years attempt to lead twenty-five thousand people to the Lord. They would build two hundred churches, develop ten "life centers" where literacy, primary health care, maternal health care, schooling, and vocational training would take place, and develop the necessary leadership to reach the people in the Periyar Region in subsequent years. With this partnership between Wichita churches and the India Gospel League, this region would be self-propagating, self-funding, and self-governing at the end of this thirty-six month period. The great thing for the Wichita group was that it would be able to complete a part of the Great Commission to an entire unreached group of people.

As we moved through the pages of my plan, I could feel those leaders becoming more interested. It wasn't long before Ron Grover moved ahead to the financial part of the plan, studied it intently, and stopped me right in the middle of one of my explanations.

"Donna," he said, "If this will only take $245,000 and we have three years to raise it, and we have this many churches working together, then we have to do it. It is reachable; it is feasible. Just think of all the people that will be won to the Lord in those three years. I think we not only *ought* to do it, but we *must* do it." What an endorsement.

The project was completed in four years. At that time the Wichita leader, Larry Wren, called for a special celebration that brought the Wichita churches together to rejoice in the fulfillment of the Great Commission in the Periyar Region. They completed their task. They empowered and trained new believers to take the Gospel to every person in that region. Now Wichita was ready to move on to a new region in India.

This plan worked not only for Wichita, but also for Cincinnati, Ohio. Other cities in the United States have asked to have such a program designed for them. More regions, more Christians, more churches, more productivity, and the Kingdom of God continues to grow.

This is another one of those transferable concepts from which you can spin other ideas and programs. It is one that is working today and one that the Lord guided us to develop. What other great programs are out there waiting for the right persons to come along so the Lord can guide them? These are mountains, but they are exciting and productive, and the view from the top is breathtaking.

From its base, a mountain looks terribly high, impossible to climb, and will surely demand a lot of work. Getting to the top is an opportunity, but it must be recognized as a mountain first, requiring much thought and preparation. If we decide to climb it, we have to take that first step and then the next and the next. It takes energy. We get tired. We lose sight of the top. We don't always know where we are or how to reach the top. Sometimes we get a great glimpse of the valley and can see how far we have come. With continued perseverance, there comes the day when we do reach the top, where we can stand and wave our arms and declare to the world that we have been successful in this endeavor. Isn't that what God wants of us? And we can be sure that he is there along side of us every step of the way.

CHAPTER 16

HARVEST: THE PATH GOES ON

I f I were a farmer looking at the harvest of my crops for a year, what would I want to see? Crops brought in on time, food on the table and in the cupboard, an attitude of celebration and satisfaction, and a sense of accomplishment and joy.

If I live to be eighty-five years old and am sitting in a rocking chair on my porch, what will I see as a harvest for the Kingdom of God? What will this entire effort amount to? Certainly I will be able to see people brought to the Lord, workers challenged and trained to carry on, an attitude of celebration and satisfaction, and a sense of accomplishment. What, however, will give me the greatest joy? I believe it is knowing my life made a difference in this world for Christ. Investing in other people, enabling thousands to see the world and choose how they can make a difference for Christ, and working with national leaders; these things bring me joy and fulfillment. Project Partner is set up to continue that legacy for others.

Through the Eyes of Christ

The years of experiencing numerous cultures has given me a global view of the world. Every choice, every action, either expresses God's truth and helps build a world to meet God's desires or contributes to a disordered and broken place to live. As poet John Donne expressed, "No man is an island." We are a part of everything and we have a commission from Christ to help change the world. In every decision and every choice we make, we either help build the Kingdom of God or we contribute to misdirection in the world and the lives of those around us. Now, this new millennium is the time for Christians to express their confidence in Christ, to set forth the banner for the Lord, and to make choices to change the world.

Seeing the world through the eyes of Christ set the direction for my life and my service to the Lord. If Chuck and I had not chosen to go to Mexico in the first place, what kind of lives would we leave behind? Because of that first step, the Lord led us through the valleys and across the mountains. He always places another mountain ahead, and he always walks with us to hold our hands and lead us on.

For me, seeing the multitudes through the eyes of Christ from the blue-coated throngs of Chinese in Beijing to the hordes of Indian people—was an unfolding process that moved me to another level of awareness of God's calling to "go into all the world." I understood that I must seek the most productive ways to serve God and work for his Kingdom. What a grander, fuller vision I now have than my first cultural encounter at the Rio Grande! The Lord gives sight and direction to those willing to move on, to risk, and to take that next step with him.

After that first Rio Grande experience, we involved ourselves with hands-on projects in missions for some thirty-five years. What we did was good. Seeing the multitudes in India and China enabled me to see a new way. As much as I wanted to be the one to share the Gospel of Jesus Christ with Hindu villagers in India or with the Chinese at Tiananmen Square, I saw through the eyes of Christ that we had to team up with local workers to really be productive—together.

The Path Goes On

What is the meaning of success? In our culture it may mean money, power, and prestige. It may involve fame and notoriety. With Christ it seems to mean faithfulness in obedience and in planting seeds along our path. He brings the increase, the harvest.

The medical ministry we began in 1989 placed us in favor with the government officials in China. We are repeatedly asked to come back. They allow us to build churches, train pastors, and encourage Christian leaders. These government officials even go with us to our church services and speak publicly to encourage the congregations to read the Bible and follow the Christian teachings. It will make better Chinese people, they say. As I understand it, Project Partner is one of only three Christian organizations that has this kind of relationship with the government. Wonderful opportunities for more involvement abound.

The path goes on!

In 1973 we took a plane-load of youth from Salem Church in Dayton, Ohio, to Guatemala. They worked to build another room onto a church building along the shore of Lake Atitlan. Nine out of the thirty-five that went on that trip are now in full-time ministry and the rest are all involved in their local churches. One among that group, Susan Hardman, now a missionary in China, said, "The trip to Guatemala confirmed for me that I wanted to give my life to missions: to live cross-culturally, to communicate in another language, to be involved in telling people about Christ. That trip thrust me out of my backyard in Trotwood, Ohio, into the front yard of the world. It gave me a taste of another culture, and that interest in experiencing other cultures has not been quenched yet."

The path goes on!

It was 1964 when I first met Enrique Cepeda. We became like family and we started helping him first with his education at Warner Pacific College in Portland, then Asbury Theological Seminary in Kentucky. He went back to Mexico and became dean of a Bible school. Later he started the "Dios es Amor" church in Mexico City. After the congregation grew to more than three hundred fifty people, he moved to Monterrey and worked with the Castillo del Rey church developing their evangelism program. A few years ago he started his own evangelism and church-planting program called Doulos International Ministries.

In 1999 alone Enrique and his teams planted more than one hundred seventy-seven churches. A church consists of fifty believers or more. His seminars reached out to more than eleven thousand participants. Nearly nine thousand people were led to Christ. Seventy pastors and leaders took training courses. His ministry is reaching across denominational lines and strengthening the body of Christians. Harvest in Mexico? Certainly. We never dreamed we would have any impact for Christ there when we started. We just followed the path that the Lord provided and now we praise him for all that happened and *continues* to happen for him.

The path goes on!

We were challenged to help a Russian national leader, Andrei Bondarenko, in 1990. He just started his tent crusades and felt the call of the Lord to make this his ministry. This year he led forty-three major evangelistic crusades in strategic cities across Russia, Latvia, and the Ukraine, such as Makeyevka, Truskavets, and Kharkov in the Ukraine; Donetsk, Murmansk, and Ulyanovsk in Russia; and Jelgave and Riga in Latvia. Each city boasts an average of two thousand people responding to the Lord at each crusade. Churches are planted, these new believers are discipled, and the new believers are continuing the harvest in those cities.

The path goes on!

I first met Samuel Stephens in 1984. His ministry has multiplied thirty-fold. With his Vision 2000 program alone which began in 1992, he and his leaders have planted more than twenty thousand churches and reached close to an estimated four hundred thousand Indian people for Christ.

His most recent outreach program, Summer Harvest, in May 2000 reached one hundred thousand people for the Lord. The children's Bible school program to three hundred thousand children developed a subsidiary program for the parents because they came too and wanted classes. To date, thirty-nine thousand pastors, teachers, and leaders are trained to continue expanding the ministry in India.

The path goes on!

China—that vast country with people waiting to hear about "a religion that helps you with your problems." What of the harvest there? In one year just short of twenty million attended evangelism meetings of various kinds including the showing of the *Jesus* film. These produced more than four million commitments to the Lord. Pastor Loo expanded his ministry to six provinces in China and is focusing on developing and training pastors and leaders among that enormous population.

The path goes on!

I worked with many other national leaders during the years, and I don't know all that is happening in their work, but I do know that the Lord caused us to meet and led us along a wonderful path with him.

The path goes on!

Another great blessing and personal ministry that has come my way is the special relationship that has developed between these national leaders and me. This is not just a working, business, or ministry relationship. It has moved into a family relationship, a confidence, trust, and love that is certainly a gift from God himself. In times of joy, they rejoice with me and I with them. In times of trouble, we share the sorrows.

Because of this "family" relationship, the Lord has given me the joy of being the American grandmother to their children. In China I participated in the "grandmother" ceremony during the double wedding of Loo's two sons. Now I am the great grandmother to their children.

In India, to Becky and Danny, Samuel and Prati's children, I have the honor of being called their American grandmother. In Nicaragua, Inez and Ali Velasquez, Jr. call me Grandma. To Enrique Cepeda's daughters, Liz, Myrna, and Melody, I have always been their American grandmother from the day they were born.

This is a unique honor that the Lord has provided for me and for which I am eternally grateful. And, as a grandmother, I have the opportunity to minister to these young people as they grow up.

The path goes on!

How has all of this influenced my own family? Those three boys who sat around the table years ago as we learned Spanish and were challenged to go to Mexico all live committed lives for the Lord. Each married a Christian, and each is deeply involved in their local church ministry. They are faithfully teaching their children God's way, and they are passing the torch to the next generation. I now have nine wonderful "American" grandchildren. As they grow old enough to understand, I am able to take each one to see what the Lord is doing on the other side of some "Rio Grande." Their worldview is expanding, and their understanding of their own choices for Christ is growing.

The path goes on!

More Mountains

As I look ahead, there's always another mountain, another view from that mountain that I didn't have before, and another faith-step. There is the incredible growth of people whose lives are touched by this ministry. There are the Christian organizations that grew from Project Partner such as the worldwide medical ministry of Caring Partners International, Guillermo Villanueva's Central American evangelism ministry, the Romanian ministry of "Jesus, the Hope of the World," Heart to Honduras, and Agape Children in Brazil, a China medical ministry, several work camp ministries, and India Gospel League's growth into a world organization.

The Lord is good. He prepares the way ahead, has his plans for us, helps us implement them, and then gives such a tremendous harvest. We need not worry about what we are going to do next but concentrate on what God can do through us right now, as we are obedient and faithful to him each step on the path.

Acts 13:36 sums it up for me: "For when David had served God's purpose in his own generation, he fell asleep." I insert my name in the place of David's and there it is—the story of Project Partner—*to serve God's purpose with the time that he allots us in life.* Neither David nor Abraham, Moses, Peter, Paul, Martin Luther, John Wesley, or D. L. Moody are alive today. This is *my* time. This is *your* time. It is *our* generation. *We* have been chosen by God to be his messengers. He gives us wonderful opportunities—wonderful mountains—just for us. Each has its summit and its victories for God. He is always with us and will never forsake us.

More glorious mountains are ahead. I can see them. Can you?

The path goes on!